Michael Wall

WOMEN LAUGHING

T0348078

OBERON BOOKS
LONDON

First published by M. Steinberg Playwrights in 1992.

This edition published in 2000 by Oberon Books Ltd.
Electronic edition published in 2013

Oberon Books Ltd
521 Caledonian Road, London N7 9RH
Tel: +44 (0) 20 7607 3637 / Fax: +44 (0) 20 7607 3629
e-mail: info@oberonbooks.com
www.oberonbooks.com

Reprinted in 2012

A catalogue record for this book is available from the British Library.

PB ISBN: 978-1-84002-156-1
E ISBN: 978-1-78319-419-3

Contents

to Nicola Wall

Michael Wall

Michael Wall (1946-1991) was born and brought up in Hereford, and came to London in the mid-Sixties, where he worked in a variety of temporary jobs before friends encouraged him to take A-levels as a first step to getting to university.

Although he had written a number of novels (unpublished), it was at York University, which he attended as a mature student in the 1970s, that he first started writing plays which were notable for their powerful language, arresting images and violence. He travelled extensively, particularly in Europe and the Far East, and much of the material for his plays was drawn from his experiences abroad. In the last few years, he was beginning to suffer from the symptoms of a brain tumour which was finally diagnosed in 1990. The birth of his daughter Nicola in 1989 provided real hope and an inspiration for his life, and in January 1990 he moved to the South of France with his partner, Lizzie Slater, but had to return to London due to his deteriorating condition. Michael spent the last days of his life in the house in Islington in which he had written most of his work. He died in London on 11 June, 1991.

It was typical of his courage and determination that, during a period in hospital, he was writing *The Use of His Hands*, an unconventional television play about illness. Towards the end of his life, he said quite simply: 'I've hardly started.'

Radio:

Japanese Style, 1982

Hiroshima: The Movie, 1985 (Winner of both Sony and Giles Cooper Awards)

The Wide-brimmed Hat, 1987

Headcrash, produced 1986 and broadcast 1993

Act of Mercy, 1988

The Last of the Lovers, 1989
Women Laughing, 1989
Doo Be Doo Be Doo, 1990
Amongst Barbarians, 1991
Runaway, 1992

Television:

Japanese Style, 1983, BBC2
Amongst Barbarians, 1990, BBC2

Stage:

Japanese Style, 1984, Belgrade Theatre, Coventry

Blue Days, 1985, Sir Richard Steele, London

Imaginary Wars in England, 1987, Duke of Cambridge, London

Amongst Barbarians, 1989, Royal Exchange Theatre, Manchester; Hampstead Theatre, London (Winner of the Mobil Playwriting Competition 1988)

Women Laughing, 1992, Royal Exchange Theatre, Manchester (Winner of the Writers' Guild Best Regional New Play 1992; Manchester Evening News Best New Play 1992); Royal Court Theatre Upstairs; Palace Theatre, Watford 1996

Resistance, 1994, The Old Red Lion Theatre, London

Rashomon, 1995: reading as part of the Moving Theatre Season, Riverside Studios

Scenes from Paradise, 1996, London New Play Festival, Riverside Studios

Publications:

Hiroshima: The Movie, Best Radio Plays of 1985, Methuen, 1985

Amongst Barbarians, Samuel French, 2000

Women Laughing, Oberon Books, 2000

INTRODUCTION

Lizzie Slater

Mourning is a sentence – a time to be endured. Mike's absence reinforces the vivid life of his characters. His death also remains more 'real' to me than anything I have experienced – to have felt the life go, that separation, the release in energy – a reality that blew up in my face: '*It's like a shadow right across my path, or a dream I can only half-remember. It makes it impossible to concentrate on anything real*' (from his radio play *Runaway*). Fifteen years of companionship and more than the odd laugh: more irrepressible laughter and keeping up with thoughts. The acoustic is strange now. I cannot remember what Mike remembered, those footsteps in the sand that Colin conjures up in *Women Laughing*. A few weeks before he died, Mike abandoned his plays and wrote some poetry:

> ...the mad world yawned
> I saw deep deep inside
> that which it was trying for untold
> centuries
> to cough up
> I felt myself, me, reeling, lost,
> lost immediately
> though I had worked so hard to prepare
> for this moment... (Poem)

He took the full impact of his own thoughts and feelings; was not prepared to cut off from pain, insisting that in the theatre, as in life, '*words convey pain*'. A theatre without words could not be a reference. The reality is in the text:

> ...Have you ever seen a mouse trying to
> box with the cat?
> I am like that, on my last and only legs,
> trying to box... (from *Catbreath*)

He lived without much protection. We travelled light, his mind racing and his mouth a riot of tastes. The tone he objected to was a self-pitying one, and bad language was not fuck-words but dishonest language. He was not violent himself, but forced himself to face all kinds of abuse; he was disgusted and tried not to flinch for *'The great men saw things we/Shield our eyes against'* (from *Catbreath*, 1991).

He took the responsibility for revealing violent impulses in his characters to make them real. When he was dying, the irony of the phrase, 'Assessment of the Activities of Living' on a questionnaire at the National Hospital did not escape him. He re-worded it *'A Englishman's Way of Dying '*; concerned with how one might die with dignity:

> My death was not discussed today
> My pain is under control.
> I cleanse and dress myself
> I use the toilet roll
> I work and play these certain hours
> Bless me how I try
> There's no change in my breathing
> Can someone tell me why?
> My sexuality is not questioned
> I mobilise at will
> I maintain a safe environment
> I'm ready for my pill.
> My anxiety is more frequent
> That cannot be denied
> Yes, I can see what you're holding
> And passing side to side
> This blurring of the vision, you see
> it's really hard to rate
> I see some things more clearly than
> others
> I can't communicate.

Something uncharacteristic had entered his thought when he asked me to tell him about the Gulf War 'when it's all over'; for he wrote as it felt to be there, wherever it was, at the time. He did not believe that he would personally be so tested, he thought he lacked the experience.

In *Women Laughing*, Tony says that '*It's the imagination, see. It won't let me be.*' Confining this play to the domestic front and the structure of marriage, he is plotting mental disturbance rather than illness. Violent thoughts are experienced as sensation; the characters fight for their lives without a death occurring. We experience thinking in action; pure mood swings that dislocate; impulses that seem to die away. *Women Laughing* is an Anatomy of Melancholy. Each character finds their own words after all. '*Life's a sod, isn't it? It's you versus terminology over fifteen rounds.*' The words clear the air.

There is a dance in *Women Laughing*, a dance that they can remember learning. As in Pina Bausch, it's concentration on action not movement. In the writing, there is a precise choreography of exchanges: one step forward, one step back. All kinds of couplings. They talk, with scarcely a break; sometimes breathless, they are compelled to speak, with an apprehension that the conversation could dry up. They've each picked a partner. With all the shambles of thought, the riot of tastes, smells, light and noise – the clamour of everyday life, there is a recognition of pain, of love and of effort to overcome inarticulacy. But we are only allowed to bask momentarily in the warmth of any sense of rightness as the thought moves on.

Shortly before he died, Mike wanted his life and work back, but finally just wanted to put his head somewhere safe. It was his imagination, see. It wouldn't let him be.

Lizzie Slater
London, 1992

Characters

all in their early thirties

COLIN

TONY

STEPHANIE

MADDY

Act One: a garden in Ealing in summer

Act Two: another garden

Women Laughing was first performed at the Royal Exchange Theatre, Manchester on 30 April 1992, with the following cast:

COLIN, Christopher Fulford
TONY, Stephen Tompkinson
STEPHANIE, Patricia Kerrigan
MADDY, Hetty Baynes

Director, Richard Wilson
Designer, Julian McGowan
Lighting, Mick Hughes
Sound, Alastair Goolden
Medical adviser, Carol Smith
Composer, Howard Davidson
Choreographer, Carol Fletcher

The play then transferred to the Royal Court Theatre Upstairs on 4 September 1992, with the following changes to the cast:

TONY, John Michie
STEPHANIE, Maggie O'Neil
MADDY, Matilda Ziegler

This publication coincided with a production by Not The National Theatre at The Wimbledon Studio Theatre, London, which opened on 19 April 2000, before embarking on a national tour. It had the following cast:

COLIN, Robin Pirongs
TONY, Jonny Hoskins
STEPHANIE, Naomi Capron
MADDY, Sarah Ingram

Director, Jeremy Raison
Designer, Michael Folkard
Choreographer, Lynne Page

ACT ONE

COLIN and TONY sitting together in the garden. COLIN is the host; TONY has recently arrived. Surrounding them, drinks and a bit of food. The garden is well cared-for, but unimaginatively done. Both men are around thirty. COLIN has a fuller figure and a larger personality than TONY. TONY seems withdrawn by comparison, a person of low spirits. It is clear that COLIN doesn't really know how to talk to him.

After a while, we hear the sound of their wives laughing – from inside the house. Perhaps their voices can be heard all the time, indistinctly, but it is when they laugh that they're especially heard. The men can't help but hear, and it makes them (COLIN in particular) feel ill-at-ease. This happens two or three times before COLIN says anything.

The women's laughter continues at intervals throughout, not only where it's referred to.

COLIN: So anyway, Tony! (*He has raised his glass.*)

TONY: Cheers.

COLIN: Cheers.

They drink. More silence.

Yes, sir.

TONY: Yeah.

COLIN: Yep. No, I was just saying to Stephanie, we must have those Catchpoles over...

TONY: Were you? What, today?

COLIN: No, no, I mean the other day, when we asked you, you know...

TONY: Oh yeah.

COLIN: ...Wouldn't say that today, would I? Because you were already coming; you were already on your way.

TONY: Yeah, we were.

COLIN: No, I mean the other day, I said, you know we don't see nearly enough of those Catchpoles.

TONY: Us?

COLIN: Yes.

TONY: Oh. Funny to think of people actually – talking about us. (*He drinks.*)

COLIN: You're happy with the beer, are you?

TONY: Sorry?

COLIN: Happy with the beer, I say the beer's alright?

TONY: Yes, I think I'll stay with the beer, thank you very much.

COLIN: Yes, only there *is* wine.

TONY: Yes, I know; I saw it.

COLIN: But beer is the best drink on a warm day, isn't it?

TONY: (*Weighing it.*) Hm...

COLIN: Wine can be nice.

TONY: Oh yes. Maddy and I have been going in for quite a lot recently.

COLIN: Oh really?

TONY: Especially the Italian variety... Soave...

COLIN: Soave, yes.

TONY: Frascati...

COLIN: Frascati.

TONY: Chianti...

COLIN: Oh, Chianti...

TONY: Verdiccio...

COLIN: Yes.

TONY: It's got that much more bite to it, I feel, than the French varieties...

COLIN: Muscadet.

TONY: Then of course, there's the question of cost.

COLIN: Ah yes, there's the rub – if you desire the Italian variety you have to pay for it.

TONY: The French is that much more expensive of course.

COLIN: Well, there you are...the *French*?

TONY: Added to which I do like a bit of sparkle in my wine.

COLIN: Have you tried that Liebfraumilch?

TONY: Yes, it's alright.

COLIN: Yes – Steph and I enjoyed a bottle the other evening. Quite enjoyable...

TONY: Very nice with fish.

COLIN: Very nice with fish. We had chops.

TONY: It's very nice with chops.

COLIN: It *was* nice. I think it might have been a bit corked.

TONY: Ah yes, well that does affect a delicate wine; I always take them back if I find them that way. Sainsbury's are very obliging like that.

COLIN: Are they? Now that wouldn't occur to me, to return a bottle of wine.

TONY: Oh yes.

COLIN: But you do that, do you?

TONY: Oh yes.

COLIN: I'd just put it down to bad luck, I think.

TONY: Oh no.

COLIN: I mean I'd *say* something, but I don't think I'd…

TONY: Oh yes. You've got to be firm – the wine industry's very sensitive these days. Very sensitive to feedback.

COLIN: Feedback, yes.

TONY: They're always trying to find out what the customer thinks.

COLIN: What, you?

TONY: Well, the customer. In this case, yeah, me.

COLIN: Well, I'd be happy to partake in a questionnaire.

TONY: Our local merchant has arranged a series of tastings – *degustation*, he calls them. It's a very good way of cultivating the palate.

COLIN: Oh, I think I sort of know what I like already. It's just finding the time, isn't it?

Pause.

They both drink.

No, I've been a confirmed beer-drinker ever since our business expanded to the States. That's why I go in for these.

TONY: Yeah, I've seen them advertised on the telly.

COLIN: I don't know, the American beers seem to have that bit of – I don't know what it is…

TONY: Bit better company, aren't they?

COLIN: Yeah. They sort of... (*He grasps the bottle.*) You know where you are with them. They don't go flat on you.

TONY: So where d'you go in the States, then? Dead Man's Gulch?

COLIN: No, Florida. Oh, you mean on business?

TONY: Well...

COLIN: No, I thought you meant on holiday, sort of thing – because Steph and I have been going there the last couple of winters.

TONY: I've always wanted to go to California – you been there?

COLIN: No. We find Florida a very high-profile winter destination...

TONY: Gambia – that's the place.

COLIN: That's Africa.

TONY: Yeah I know, but more and more people are going there, so I hear.

COLIN: I don't know, maybe they are.

TONY: I don't fancy Africa, though. I don't think I'd feel safe, you know what I mean?

COLIN: I know exactly what you mean.

TONY: It's all very well having good beaches but it's not much good if you're shot dead the minute you step off them, is it?

COLIN: Or eaten by a tiger.

TONY: That's right. Well, you got to think of these things – I mean if you're paying good money. Also, I mean the language: I know Africans speak English, but with them you feel somehow they don't really want to, you know?

COLIN: They're doing you a big favour, sort of thing?

TONY: Yeah.

COLIN: No, that's what I really admire about the old Yanks – all the competition that goes on out there. Like they all really want your business. I admire that: they really know when they've got a product and how to go about marketing it. Not like us – we gave away the Hovercraft; we give everything away.

TONY: We haven't even managed to put up a Disneyland.

COLIN: Ah, it's ridiculous. Because the businessman is despised in this country, that's what it is. He's looked down on, 'cos he's in trade. Whereas in America he's God. They know what they're doing Stateside. I mean they owe more money than most countries will ever have.

TONY: Unfortunately my business only takes me to the European markets as yet, although we are hoping to expand.

COLIN: I should hope so, Tony. There's no point being in business if you don't want to expand, is there?

TONY: Branch out sort of thing.

COLIN: That's right.

TONY: Yeah. Very, um, competitive, the Americans.

COLIN: Of course they are.

TONY: Yes, sort of protectionist, really.

COLIN: Well, it's like everything else, isn't it? You wouldn't respect it if it came without a fight, would you?

TONY: No.

COLIN: It wouldn't be worth having.

TONY: The Japs get in there, don't they?

COLIN: Japs? Ah, they're fucking mad, aren't they? All very nice and polite on the surface and everything, but give them a business opening and they react like they've been thrown a lump of red meat.

TONY: Well, you know, they got a different ethic. 'He who hesitates is…'

COLIN: Yeah, but you've got to *live*, haven't you? I mean there's more to life than chasing the bloody dollar.

TONY: (*Gloomily.*) Yeah.

Pause.

The women are heard laughing.

COLIN: What, so you're not doing very well at the moment, then?

TONY: Oh yes! No, we're doing alright. It's just that we're not quite sure of, you know.

COLIN: Not quite sure you want to go with the…

TONY: We're not quite sure.

COLIN: Yeah.

Well, it's always a good idea to kick it around a bit, you know.

TONY: Ah – that's an American expression there!

COLIN: Is it? Yes, I'm very impressionable.

TONY: I thought so.

COLIN: No, people sometimes look at me a bit, you know; they think I'm sort of…

TONY: Sort of putting 'em on.

COLIN: Yeah. But I'm not; it's just that they've sort of rubbed off on me. I was like that at school… Kids always used to say to me – Eh, Colin, do him, do her, 'cos I was a natural mimic.

TONY: Really? Can land you in trouble, that sort of thing.

COLIN: Oh no.

TONY: Especially with foreigners. They don't understand.

Pause.

COLIN: So how's the car running?

TONY: Oh alright; no complaints.

COLIN: Metro, isn't it?

TONY: Regata, actually.

COLIN: Yeah, I knew it was a small car.

TONY: It's a family saloon, not that small.

COLIN: No, I was thinking in terms of…

TONY: Not in cost, I hope.

COLIN: Costing you a packet, is it? They do, these foreign cars.

TONY: No it's alright, it's…

COLIN: It's the parts.

TONY: It's just that the parts are so expensive.

COLIN: This is it.

TONY: The fuel pump went on it…

COLIN: They always go on Italian cars, Tony, didn't you know that…?

TONY: One hundred and twenty-six pounds fifty…

COLIN sucks his breath.

The mechanic said to me if this had been an English car…

COLIN: Half the cost.

TONY: It would have cost you half as much.

COLIN: Yes.

TONY: I queried it with the AA.

COLIN: No, no, that's what it costs to run a foreign car these days.

TONY: What are you driving?

COLIN: A Citroën.

TONY: Start alright?

COLIN: When it feels like it.

TONY: Beats me how they fork out all that money or advertising and they can't come up with a car that actually starts.

COLIN: (*Suddenly cross.*) Yes, well, what are they laughing about in there?

TONY: Ah… (*He waves an airy hand in their direction.*)

COLIN: What?

TONY: Sorry?

COLIN: What does that mean? (*Imitates the gesture.*)

TONY: Well, I mean – I don't know.

COLIN: They haven't stopped. Did you two have a drink on the way?

TONY: No. We did have a gin and…

COLIN: When you arrived, yes, I know; I'm talking about on the way here.

TONY: No, there's no point drinking on the way when…

COLIN: Anyway, are they coming out here or not?

TONY: I expect they'll come out when they're ready.

COLIN: Well, there's no need for them to stay in there, is there? The food was all prepared before you arrived and we're out here. I mean why do they want to stay in there – when we're out here?

TONY: Beats me.

COLIN: It beats me.

TONY: Well, it's women, isn't it?

COLIN: What is?

TONY: Well.

COLIN: What?

TONY: You know.

COLIN: *What?*

TONY: You know – they find anything, don't they? They can talk about anything. It's like with food. You come home late at night, there's nothing in the fridge, you say, come on let's go and get a Chinese; they say, no I can whip something up easy. Whip something up; that's what they say. A few eggs, a bit of old Spam – there you are. It's the same with talking. They can go on for hours about nothing whatsoever.

COLIN: Well, it must be about *something.*

TONY: Well, it is and it isn't, you know.

COLIN: It must be about kids.

TONY: Yeah, they go on about babies for hours, guaranteed.

COLIN: I know, but I don't know why they're laughing so much.

TONY: It's a mystery, isn't it? I mean it wouldn't be funny to us, would it?

COLIN: Well, not if it's about what the kids did today, no.

TONY: Well, there you are.

COLIN: (*Not satisfied.*) Hmm.

TONY: Stephanie hold her drink, can she?

COLIN: Oh – not so bad.

TONY: Maddy's like a sieve. I always find that a bit of a turn-off, actually. A drunken woman.

COLIN: Oh, yeah.

TONY: Like they're trying to compete with the blokes. You know.

COLIN: Yeah.

TONY: And there's no way they can. Because their whatsanames are different. Their constitutions. I mean a monkey would get drunk a lot quicker than an elephant.

COLIN: Yes.

Pause.

They both drink their beer.

TONY: If you'll excuse me a moment...

COLIN: Yes, yes...

TONY: I must just go for a piss.

COLIN: That's the thing about beer, Tony.

TONY: I know, but I quite enjoy pissing, you know.

COLIN: Oh yeah.

TONY: If it's convenient, sort of thing. You can sort of – take stock, can't you?

COLIN: Take stock, yes.

TONY: Hm. See you.

COLIN: See you.

TONY goes off.

COLIN lights a cigar.

STEPHANIE and MADDIE come on. They bring with them various items of food – crêpes especially. They are laughing, and when they see COLIN sitting there, looking at them, their laughter is redoubled. He watches them for a while, waiting for them to tell him what they're laughing about. But they don't.

Okay, I'll buy it.

STEPHANIE: What?

COLIN: Whatever it is that's so wonderfully amusing – I'll buy it.

They look at one another and start laughing again.

STEPHANIE: (*Laughing.*) ...Says he'll 'buy' it... He doesn't buy anything...

COLIN: No, it must be absolutely hilarious; Tony and I have been sitting out here, truly amazed that you can find so much to laugh about.

STEPHANIE: (*Laughing as she says it.*) Colin, you've let the ice melt.

COLIN: I suspect it would have melted anyway.

MADDY: Are you alright out here, Colin?

COLIN: Yes thank you, Maddy; thank you for asking. Just wondering when you were going to condescend to actually join us. After all, I was under the illusion that this was a 'party' – i.e. a gathering of four persons...

Oh, come on, what's so funny?

STEPHANIE: We've just found out something.

MADDY: Oh, don't tell him!

COLIN: Oh, you have, haven't you? Well, it must be absolutely hilarious – do please share it.

STEPHANIE: I'm going to tell him.

MADDY: Oh, alright.

STEPHANIE: Otherwise, you know, it's not really very fair, is it?

MADDY: No, I suppose not.

COLIN: I'm very impressed so far.

STEPHANIE: Keep this wine in the shade…

COLIN: Never mind that; come on. I feel like a laugh.

They both laugh again.

Oh!

STEPHANIE: No, alright – alright – we just found out, Maddy and I…that Tony is seeing a psychiatrist!

COLIN: Yes? And the punch line of this particular anecdote?

STEPHANIE: Well, I agree, it's not funny until you realise that – well, that you are seeing a psychiatrist too.

MADDY: Oh, it's not really funny, is it?

COLIN: Oh come, come, Madeleine – it's obviously *very* funny. It's had the two of you in stitches in there for half an hour.

STEPHANIE: Well, it just struck us that way. Because she told me about Tony, and I – well, I remembered about you, and Doctor Herzenberger.

They laugh.

COLIN: Herzen*berg*, actually.

STEPHANIE: But you're both under analysis, you see.

COLIN: Yes, I see, but – I still don't see what's so side-splitting about it.

STEPHANIE: Well, it is rather, Colin, because – Oh, I can't explain it; it just sort of tickled us, didn't it?

COLIN: Hilarious.

STEPHANIE: But I think it's probably because here you are, the two of you, sitting out here, talking about God knows what, and neither of you knows the other is having analysis.

COLIN: Well, it's not the sort of thing you talk about, is it?

MADDY: Yes, you just think of women, I suppose. You don't associate it with men so much, do you? I think that's what set us off really.

COLIN: Thank you for explaining it to me, Maddy.

STEPHANIE: Yes – it's just us bored old housewives as a rule, isn't it?

COLIN: Alright, I'll buy that too. So, um, why is he? Why is Tony seeing a psychiatrist?

MADDY: Well, he's actually finished with psychiatry now.

COLIN: Oh, he's 'finished', has he? Get him!

MADDY: No, he's moved on to group therapy. (*She stifles a laugh.*)

STEPHANIE: Just like you, Colin.

COLIN: I doubt that, Stephanie.

STEPHANIE: He lets it all hang out on Tuesdays and Thursdays.

COLIN: Christ, that's a lot of therapy. Well, I expect it's something he's – thought through, sort of thing. I still don't see what's so… But what's he going for? I mean I always thought Tony was, you know, really well-adjusted. Mister Normal.

MADDY: Ah, you don't know him, Colin.

COLIN: Not as you know him, I grant you, but…

MADDY: He was having these panic attacks.

COLIN: Oh yeah? What are they?

STEPHANIE: They sound very similar to yours actually, Colin.

COLIN: I doubt that Stephanie. I doubt that they're anything like as bad as mine; there are many…

MADDY: Well, it wasn't the only thing, you know.

She leaves it at that.

COLIN: Well, I must say I think it's completely unresponsible of you both to be standing there, laughing at our problems – if indeed problems they be.

STEPHANIE: 'Irresponsible', darling.

COLIN: Yes. That's what I said.

STEPHANIE: You said 'unresponsible'.

COLIN: Well now, how could I have said that when there's no such word?

STEPHANIE: I don't know, but you did.

COLIN: I think I know what I said, thank you. Well, I must say, this little episode has done more than anything to convince me that women have absolutely no moral fibre. It's completely missing from their make-up. To be – laughing at their husbands' misfortune – if indeed misfortune it be – I'm sorry I think that's just plain immoral.

STEPHANIE: You can eat those to be going on with.

COLIN: Oh, you're going back in now, are you? Charming, isn't it – you explode your pathetic little bomb and piss off back to the kitchen.

STEPHANIE: We know our place.

They go. On the way they pass TONY coming back. They laugh. TONY is quiet and thoughtful now. COLIN watches him warily.

COLIN: Alright?

TONY: Yes thanks.

COLIN: We were honoured with a brief visit.

TONY: Oh – yeah. Did they tell you what they were laughing about?

COLIN: No. Who cares?

TONY: Are they starting to bring out the, um…? D'you think we should go and help them?

COLIN: No, let them do it. I did all the shopping.

TONY: We supposed to eat these pancakes?

COLIN: I don't know. They're crêpes actually.

TONY: (*Looking at them.*) Oh. Are you alright?

COLIN: Me? Yes. Why?

TONY: I don't know – you seemed to have assumed a contemplative demeanour.

COLIN: That's funny; that's exactly what I thought *you'd* assumed.

TONY: Oh. (*He sniffs and continues to look at the crêpes.*)

COLIN: (*Half to himself.*) Women.

TONY: What?

COLIN: Hm?

TONY: What about 'women'?

COLIN: Oh, nothing; just thinking.

Pause.

TONY: Well, what were you 'thinking' about them? I mean
what aspect?

COLIN: Well, all aspects really.

TONY: Oh.

COLIN: I mean… (*He shapes his argument with his hands,
gives up and lets them drop. He shakes his head.*) Cheers, eh?

TONY: Cheers, yeah.

COLIN: Ah, that's good.

TONY: (*Drinking.*) Yep. Well, whatever it was you said to
them it's had the effect, anyway.

COLIN: What effect?

TONY: It's stopped them laughing.

COLIN: Oh yes.

TONY: What were they laughing about?

COLIN: I told you, I don't know.

TONY: Well, they're not doing it any more. You must
have put a right old damper on things. Is it 'damper' or
'dampener'? I never know.

COLIN: I wouldn't use either.

TONY: No, it always worries me, that, actually. It always
worries me when I disuse a word. And then there's

those occasions when you discover what a word means and you realise with that horrible numb feeling, you know, that you've been using it wrong for *years*. Absolutely years. It's all out of proportion, but it gets to you somehow; even gives you sleepless nights – you know what I mean?

COLIN: (*A beat.*) You shouldn't worry.

TONY: No, I know, it's silly, but…

COLIN: No, no, seriously, you shouldn't worry. Nobody thanks you for worrying.

TONY: That's true.

COLIN: I mean most people, they just trample. They trample and – stamp over everything, all feelings, all… Ah.

TONY: (*Looking at him.*) Yes.

COLIN: I mean I get uptight about silly things too. But what I'm saying is – they all come right in the end, don't they? Hm?

TONY: Yeah.

COLIN: Yes. Of course they do.

TONY: Are we supposed to eat these, Colin?

COLIN: Staying on the beer, are you?

TONY: I think so, if that's…

COLIN: I mean you haven't got to, just because I am. You already told me you're a wine-drinker by inclination.

TONY: No, no, beer's a nice drink on a warm day.

COLIN: Okay. (*Drinks.*) Alright.

They both drink.

The women are heard laughing again.

TONY: I wonder what's got into them today. Still. It's sort of nice, don't you think? The sound of women laughing – it's a sort of tinkling sound, isn't it? Chiming. Like the sound of cattle-bells on a high Alpine pasture. It makes you think of – innocence.

COLIN: I forget whether you smoke?

TONY: Mm? Oh, thank you. I'll smoke a cigar any day of the week.

COLIN: I got them in Amsterdam.

TONY: Ah, that's a good place for cigars. Where else? Hamburg; they have lovely Havanas. Brussels.

They light up.

There on business, were you?

COLIN: What?

TONY: In Amsterdam on business, were you? On business, in Amsterdam?

COLIN: Yes I was. Why?

TONY: Oh – it's just that I thought you were, you know?

COLIN: No.

TONY: No, it's just that I thought you were more involved in the US market, at the present moment.

COLIN: We are. But we also do business in Europe.

TONY: Yeah.

COLIN: We are part of a... (*Attempts a vast, complex gesture.*)

TONY: Oh yes, so are we.

COLIN: Besides, it's never a chore to visit Amsterdam. A most relaxing city, I always find.

TONY: Especially round that red-light district, eh!

COLIN: …The art of Van Gogh, Rembrandt. Have you visited the new Van Gogh Museum there?

TONY: No I haven't.

COLIN: Wonderful place. Wonderful place to view art. They must have spent a lot of money on it and every time I go there, you know, I can't help remarking on the irony of the situation – there was Van Gogh; he sold one picture in his life – one picture, and all that terrible suffering – and here's this lavish monument.

TONY: Who do you remark upon it to?

COLIN: What?

TONY: No, you said you always remark on it – I just wondered who you remark upon it to, that's all. 'To *whom* you remark it?'

COLIN: To no one. To myself.

TONY: Ah, I see. I thought – I thought perhaps there was a little more to these 'business trips' than met the eye. He said leaning forward, his voice pregnant with innuendo.

COLIN: I speak to myself sometimes.

TONY: Oh, so do I! The stares I get on the Tube, eh?

COLIN: A little eccentricity on one's make-up is essential, don't you find?

TONY: Absolutely – where would you be without it? Are we supposed to eat these, do you think?

COLIN: Eccentricity as opposed to… I mean, keeping it in proportion.

TONY: Oh yes.

COLIN: So you get stared at on the Tube, do you?

TONY: I don't know; I don't suppose so. It just feels like it, you know.

COLIN: In your imagination, sort of thing?

TONY: Yeah. I don't think anyone cares really. All wrapped up in their own worlds, aren't they?

COLIN: Cares about what? I mean what do you do?

TONY: Oh, only mumble a bit, like. Don't foam at the mouth or anything!

COLIN: No, no...

TONY: Look, the ants are going to get these – I'll put 'em up here, shall I?

COLIN: Eat one.

TONY: I think I will actually.

COLIN: Go on.

TONY: 'Cos it's better than the ants eating 'em, isn't it?

COLIN: Marginally, Tony, yes.

TONY: Or should I wait until the girls come?

COLIN: They're probably scoffing them in there.

TONY: Ummm...

COLIN: You make your mind up and you eat one – what could be simpler?

TONY: It's the making up of the mind, isn't it?

COLIN: Go on, here, for goodness' sake.

TONY: 'Cos they'll go cold, won't they? Okay – what about you?

COLIN: I'll just smoke this.

TONY: Got mushrooms inside 'em, Colin.

COLIN: Yeah, well they're crêpes.

TONY: I was going to say – a pancake as such doesn't usually have things inside it, does it?

COLIN: It does in the States. Ask for a pancake over there and you get a full-course meal.

TONY: (*Eating.*) Got big sandwiches too, haven't they?

COLIN: Cor, the sandwiches. In New York especially. The Big Apple.

TONY: What, apple sandwiches?

COLIN: No, no, that's what they call New York. No, you ask for a sandwich over there, you have to ask for a brown bag, you can't possibly eat it all.

TONY: A brown bag – what's that? To be sick into?

COLIN: No, to take it home with you. That what you can't eat.

TONY: Oh, I see.

COLIN breathes deeply, exhausted at having to explain.

Brown bag, eh? I shall have to remember that…
(*Eating.*) Very nice. They making a whole pile, are they?

Pause.

The women are heard laughing again.

– What are you looking at me like that for?

COLIN: Like what?

TONY: All sort of – (*He makes a face.*)

COLIN: I wasn't looking like that.

TONY: You were.

COLIN: I wasn't. I *couldn't* look like that. Make me feel like Boris Karloff.

TONY: I mean shouldn't I be eating these really?

COLIN: Tony. I really do want you to eat the crêpes.

TONY: I don't want to eat them all! Don't make out I'm trying to eat them all. I just thought you were thinking you'd rather I waited until the ladies joined us.

COLIN: No.

TONY: Alright.

COLIN: Interesting. It just goes to show, that, doesn't it? You see, I wasn't thinking anything of the kind there, Tony...

TONY: Oh well, fair enough.

COLIN: No, but it's interesting because you construed that I was.

TONY: No, no, I was just...

COLIN: It's a terrifying thing – that after four thousand years of civilisation little mistakes can still be made. Between friends and acquaintances. So it's little wonder that governments behave the way they do. I was thinking about something quite, quite different.

TONY: Yeah, it's so funny, isn't it?

COLIN: And as for the face you accused me of making...

TONY: No, no, it wasn't an accusation...

COLIN: Well, suggested I was making...

TONY: No, it's just the way you were looking at that moment. Just the way it caught my eye, you know.

COLIN: How's your beer?

TONY: (*Eating.*) Oh fine, thanks, I'm alright.

COLIN: Alright?

TONY: Yep.

COLIN: Cheers.

TONY: (*Eating.*) Cheers. Garden's looking very nice.

COLIN: Hm?

TONY: The garden. I say the garden's looking very nice, the garden.

COLIN: Oh yeah. It has its moments, doesn't it?

TONY: Maddy does our garden really. Gives her something to do, you know. I think she gets a bit cheesed-off sat at home all day so it provides a pleasant diversion. I mean kids are alright but you have to talk such rubbish to them, don't you? You have to wait sixteen years before you can converse with them and even then it's 'Eh, Mum, I got pimples!' or '*Why* can't I stay out tonight?' We went over to that garden centre in Alexandra Palace and bought some trellises – they were twenty pounds cheaper
than exactly the same ones at that place in Highgate. Ridiculous, isn't it? Anyway, we got some Russian vine and – I don't know what else really – clematis, could it be? – anyway we bought all these rambling plants and we're growing them up the trellises.

COLIN: Oh, they're all daffodils to me, old chap, except roses.

TONY: Well, we decided it was time we had a little bit more privacy, you know, from over the back. You're alright here; they can't see over, but you know, at our place – they can see right over, see everything you're doing, sort of thing. It does make you sort of tense sometimes, you know? I mean in your own garden. Plus they've got a rather unruly dog which keeps jumping over the wall, so we put up the trellis and it can't do it now. And we can grow stuff on it – quite nice, some of that vine, you know, and it doesn't half grow fast. Sort of creeper stuff it is really. And you can train it; it isn't just random. It's already knee-height and we only bought it last Sunday. No, it was Saturday 'cos we had to go over to Maddy's mum on the Sunday, that's it. Shall I eat this other one as well only it's a shame to let them go cold?

COLIN: Please do, Tony.

TONY: Alright, you talked me into it. (*Eats.*) Mm, this one appears to have leek in it. I never thought I liked leek, but this is quite nice. You're doing it again.

COLIN: What?

TONY: You're looking at me like Boris Karloff again.

COLIN: Oh God, what am I supposed to do? Smile all the time, like an idiot.

TONY: No, not if there's nothing to smile at.

COLIN: I'll look over here.

TONY: No, no, it doesn't matter.

COLIN: But I'm not doing it!

TONY: No, it's probably just my imagination. Probably because I'm talking too much. I do talk too much. I do talk too much sometimes – Maddy's always having to take me aside.

COLIN: You're not talking too much. It's probably something you need to do.

TONY: Yeah, it must be that G and T you gave us when we came in.

COLIN: Well, you did have two...

TONY: Oh yeah, so I did...

COLIN: And they were quite strong. It's my practice to serve guests a stiff drink upon arrival.

TONY: And a stiffer one when you want them to push off, eh?

COLIN: No, no…

TONY: It's alright. I'm only kidding. Mm, that was nice.

Pause.

Meanwhile the women are heard laughing again. Over the laughter, COLIN makes a throat-clearing sound of irritation.

Eh, you ever heard women talking together? I mean when they think they can't be heard? Cor, the language! Ten times worse than us, I'll tell you.

COLIN: Worse than us?

TONY: Worse than men.

COLIN: Oh men, I thought you meant us. What, you mean it's profane?

TONY: Profane – that's a nice way of putting it.

COLIN: They tell me the graffiti in women's lavatories is much worse than men's.

TONY: Oh, they tell you that, do they?

COLIN: Well, I mean I…

TONY: It's far worse. And some of the drawings – phoo! We just don't have any idea.

COLIN: Any idea of what?

TONY: What goes on in their minds. How they think. I mean, for example, do they think about sex more than we do? I reckon they do.

COLIN: (*Darkly.*) I know Stephanie does.

TONY: And I hate it when women complain we're always looking at them. You know, like, we're staring at their

legs and everything. Pressurising them, they call it.
I mean, at least we're open about it, aren't we?

COLIN: Mm.

TONY: Not like them. Because *they* look at us, don't they?

COLIN: Men, you mean?

TONY: Yeah, men, us. They look at us – but with them
it's sort of sneaky, out the corner of the eye, sort of
thing. You can catch 'em at it sometimes; doesn't half
embarrass them.

COLIN: Catch them looking at you.

TONY: Yeah.

COLIN: In the street?

TONY: Yeah.

COLIN: They'll be prostitutes.

TONY: No, no, ordinary women. Maybe they don't look
at you.

COLIN: I don't know.

TONY: Funny, I catch 'em out quite often.

COLIN: Yes, you said. They look at you, you're saying,
but not at me – or the general man?

TONY: Don't know about the general man; I've never
met him.

COLIN: Yes well, I was alluding more to the mind,
actually, Tony.

TONY: Oh sorry, usual mistake…

COLIN: What goes on in the mind of woman.

TONY: What woman?

COLIN: The general woman.

TONY: Oh yes.

COLIN: How they think. How they perceive things. How they…

TONY: What makes 'em tick.

COLIN: Yes, that's a succinct way of putting it.

TONY: Yeah, it's a good expression, that, isn't it? I think people *do* tick, you know. I know I do. I'm like a bomb. One of these days I'm going to explode. BOOM!

Inside, the women have heard this. They start laughing again.

Well, I'm glad it amuses someone anyway.

COLIN: They are completely over the top.

TONY: My mother used to laugh a lot.

COLIN: (*Warily.*) Your mother?

TONY: Yeah, she had a terrific sense of humour. Used to do impersonations of people. She could do all the family – except my aunt in Scarborough; she was undoable.
What was your mother like?

COLIN: My mother? Why?

TONY: I don't know, I…

COLIN: Anyway, she's still alive.

TONY: Oh yes, I thought she was.

COLIN: Why d'you ask, anyway?

TONY: Well, no, I just wondered – was she an amusing woman?

COLIN: Well actually, I must tell you I find that a rather strange question, Tony. You don't usually associate *mothers* with a sense of humour.

TONY: Oh I do.

COLIN: As a matter of fact – since you ask – yes, she did laugh quite a lot.

TONY: Ah, you see!

COLIN: But she wasn't typical – she was rather unique, my mother. Rather a special woman, as a matter of fact.

TONY: Well, she must have been if she laughed a lot.

COLIN: Well, my father gave her plenty to laugh at.

TONY: Funny man, was he?

COLIN: Unwittingly, yes. When she wasn't laughing she was crying.

TONY: Yes, I know, brimful of emotions. House full of men, was it?

COLIN: I did have a couple of brothers, yes.

TONY: Ah you see. Poor old dear.

COLIN: (*A bit nettled.*) I do see her, you know.

TONY: Oh, that's nice.

COLIN: I go every week to her twilight home in Hendon.

TONY: Oh yes. Her what?

COLIN: It's a rest-home. I call it a twilight home; it's an example of the terminology I picked up in the States.

TONY: Does she use a walking frame, yeah?

COLIN: No she doesn't. She's quite hale and hearty as a matter of fact.

TONY: Well, sometimes these homes can bring out the best in old folk.

COLIN: Well, it was certainly better than that block of flats she was living in…

TONY: Hendon – you go along the North Circular, do you?

COLIN: Yes. As a rule.

TONY: Terrible road.

COLIN: Well, it's improved no end since the advent of the M25.

TONY: Oh yes.

COLIN: Less heavy vehicles, for example.

TONY: But it's still a terrible road.

COLIN: Yes but nothing's going to stop me seeing my mother, is it?

TONY: They ought to widen it around Golders Green there – knock down some of these houses, that hospital, put in an extra lane each way.

COLIN: Trouble is, once you knock down the houses – well, you're just left with gardens, aren't you?

TONY: Yeah, I know what you mean, because then the road abuts straight onto the gardens rather than the houses, and that's no one's idea of a road.

COLIN: They could get round it by rebuilding the houses in what is now the gardens, so the road would still abut onto the houses…

COLIN/TONY: (*Together.*) As it does at the moment.

TONY: True.

COLIN: It's all very well, people wanting gardens, but
I mean this is a capital city. There isn't the space.
In Germany everyone lives in flats.

COLIN: In Amsterdam they don't even live in that.

TONY: That's right.

COLIN: People can't have everything. I just can't
understand the anti-road lobby in this country, Tony;
they want their cars but they resist all efforts to improve
the roads.
It makes me really angry.

TONY: Yeah. I think I'll eat this last crêpe.

*The women are coming across the lawn. STEPHANIE is
pushing a squeaky trolley. They can be heard, chatting and
laughing as they approach.*

STEPHANIE: Yoo hoo!

COLIN: Oh watch out…

STEPHANIE: Hello there! On holiday, are you?

MADDY: Mind if we join you?

COLIN: Ah, so you've condescended to join us at last,
have you?

STEPHANIE: Yeah, we thought we'd lighten the gloom,
didn't we, Maddy?

COLIN: What d'you bring that old trolley out for?

STEPHANIE: It saves you making repeated journeys to
the kitchen, Colin.

COLIN: It's got squeaky wheels.

STEPHANIE: So have you but I still use you from time
to time.

The women laugh.

TONY: Sounds like they're bringing their humour out here, Colin.

COLIN: Oh, is that what you'd call it? I wouldn't go that far personally.

STEPHANIE: Oh, you've eaten all the crêpes, Colin – I thought you had no appetite...

TONY: No, I, um...

COLIN: It was him...

MADDY: I'm glad you ate them, Colin, because I'm afraid there was leeks in one of them and Tony doesn't like leeks, do you?

TONY: Well, as a matter of...

MADDY: Sorry.

STEPHANIE: Oh, don't apologise for him, Maddy. We start apologising for them we'll be here all day.

COLIN: About the crêpes – it wasn't...

STEPHANIE: Put that cigar out and pass round the plates please.

COLIN: Right. Although, if you don't mind, I believe I can smoke the cigar *and* pass round the plates at the same time. I'm only marginally dyslexic.

MADDY: What does he say he is?

STEPHANIE: Well, put it in the ashtray.

COLIN: I'm keeping it in my mouth – and I'm passing round the plates – okay?

MADDY: He looks a bit like Groucho Marx with that, doesn't he?

STEPHANIE: He does a bit, doesn't he?

44

COLIN coughs and splutters.

Ah, told you!

TONY: Do we eat this first, or...?

MADDY: Wait a bit, can't you?

TONY: No, I was just wondering what to put on my plate, that's all.

MADDY: Haven't you heard of women first?

STEPHANIE: Oh-oh, no talking for thirty seconds...

A giant aircraft passes low overhead, drowning out all sound. It takes some time.

COLIN: ...absolutely free of charge, but we said no, didn't we, Steph?

STEPHANIE: Did we, Colin, yes.

TONY: What?

COLIN: What, you want me to say all that again?

TONY: I couldn't hear, could I?

STEPHANIE: You must remember that people outside the Ealing area don't have ears that are attuned to landing aeroplanes, Colin.

COLIN: Alright! No, all I said was – the BAA offered to let us have free double-glazing, plus free installation and everything...

STEPHANIE: But we said no. Will you pass the salad cream, please?

TONY: What d'you say no for?

STEPHANIE: Don't ask me, love. Thank you – and the vinegar...

COLIN: Because – I don't approve of it, Tony. Double-glazing disrupts the original features of the house...

STEPHANIE: Can only be a good thing then, can't it?

COLIN: …Look at this house. Look. Can you imagine what effect double-glazing would have on those windows?

TONY: Make it a lot quieter. I couldn't live with that noise.

STEPHANIE: Oh, he just turns the telly up louder, Tony.

MADDY: Anyway, you can't have double-glazing in your garden, can you?

STEPHANIE: Very true, Maddy.

COLIN: It'll be quiet enough in the grave, thank you very much.

STEPHANIE: Going soon, are you? Are you having some of this, Maddy? There were meant to be crêpes for starters but I'm afraid my husband's scoffed the lot.

COLIN: I didn't…

STEPHANIE: Oh look – don't let the ants get in the smoked ham.

MADDY: Have you ever seen ants carrying a piece of ham? We saw that, didn't we, Tony? Where was that?

TONY: You're thinking of that Walt Disney film.

MADDY: No, it was in Portugal. Do you remember the ants in Portugal?

TONY: Yes I do.

Pause.

They all eat.

STEPHANIE: (*Eating.*) Mm, this AIDS advert on the telly – have you seen it?

MADDY: Ooh yes.

STEPHANIE: It's horrible, isn't it?

MADDY: Well, I just have to turn over.

COLIN: It's not an AIDS advert; it's just the opposite. It's...

STEPHANIE: But can you imagine anything worse than sharing a needle? They've no need to warn me like that.

COLIN: They're not aiming at *you.*

STEPHANIE: Yeah, but they're hitting me, aren't they? Every night.

COLIN: It's not aimed at you, at us – it's aimed at them. Out there. All those poor millions of inadequate people who are completely beyond our ken.

MADDY: Oh, I used to like that, Beyond Our Ken.

STEPHANIE: And it isn't fair. Just because there happens to be a minority of people who inject themselves with dirty needles and all that, we don't want it rammed down our throats, do we?

MADDY: Yeach!

TONY: Can I have another piece of pie, please?

MADDY: No, I do think they go too far sometimes.

COLIN: Well, Tony, it does look as though we're going to have to endure a definite lowering of the intellectual tone from now on.

TONY: (*Eating.*) Are we?

STEPHANIE: Why? D'you mean 'cos we've come? What a cheek. Can you pass the salad?

COLIN: Here. You now have the entire meal clustered about you...

STEPHANIE: Oh yes I do, don't I?

COLIN: You look like a deity with all her offerings.

MADDY: Does your husband always talk like this?

STEPHANIE: It's only showing off.

COLIN: It's always 'showing off', isn't it? That's exactly what my mother used to say.

STEPHANIE: She still does. No, he's talking more this way recently, ever since he started his Open University course.

MADDY: Oh, I like those programmes; I find them very educational.

TONY: Bit boring, aren't they? They could be showing films that time of night.

STEPHANIE: (*Eating.*) A deity. Yes. Queen of Ealing – it doesn't quite go, does it?

TONY: So what were you laughing at all that time, you two?

COLIN: Who cares?

STEPHANIE: We were laughing at a number of things, Tony, a whole range of subjects. Didn't Colin tell you?

TONY: No, he said…

COLIN: Why don't you fill your mouth even more, darling? Here – try some of this baguette.

STEPHANIE: Ooh, get off!

MADDY: Is it called a baguette in this country?

STEPHANIE: You hurt me then.

COLIN: Good.

MADDY: …That's the actual French name, isn't it? '*Un baguette, s'il vous plaît*'.

STEPHANIE: There's an aggression in you, Colin.

COLIN: Only a normal one, Steph.

STEPHANIE: ...I think it's something we should talk about with an interested party.

COLIN: Yeah well, no one's interested, are they?

STEPHANIE: Tony is, aren't you, Tony?

TONY: (*Eating.*) What?

STEPHANIE: You're interested in Colin's aggression.

TONY: Oh – yeah.

MADDY: Why can't you listen?

TONY: I was listening; I was eating.

MADDY: Well, why can't you do the two at the same time?

COLIN: Yes well...

A cork pops.

White wine anyone?

TONY: Yeah. Let's have a look.

MADDY: Don't be so rude.

COLIN: Oh, sorry, am I not showing the label? Here, that's better.

TONY: Ah yes.

COLIN: There you are, you see – the vineyard, the year, the part of meadow, the '*mise en bouteille...*'

STEPHANIE: The supermarket...

MADDY: Is he doing French at the Open University?

TONY: That will do nicely thank you; you may serve it.

COLIN: Would M'sieur like it over his head or in his lap?

TONY: In there will do nicely.

STEPHANIE: Colin, I'm sorry but you are definitely being aggressive.

COLIN: Oh, *I'm* being aggressive, am I? (*He laughs curiously again.*)

STEPHANIE: Tony was only showing a bit of breeding by being interested in the label.

COLIN: Yeah well, a camel shows breeding, doesn't it?

STEPHANIE: Now fill Maddy's glass up; you might have gone to her in the first place.

MADDY: Oh, not filled... Ooh, stop! When!

COLIN: Oh sorry.

STEPHANIE: (*Softly.*) You've spilt it.

MADDY: It's alright; I can sort it – suck it off the top. (*She slurps.*)

TONY: You know what the word for that is? On the top of her glass? Miniscus.

MADDY: Is it? He's ever so good with words, Tony, you know. He's like a phosphorous.

COLIN: A what?

TONY: I think she means Thesaurus.

STEPHANIE: Oh!

MADDY: Oh, of course! Phosphorous!

The women laugh.

COLIN: Well done; you've set them off again.

TONY: Ah, leave them. It's sort of nice.

COLIN: Oh yes – it 'tinkles', doesn't it? Reminds you of your mother.

TONY: Funny, I seem to have drunk that already.

COLIN: Really? How amazing. You must let me help you to some more.

MADDY: I'll be all day with this.

TONY: That's not a bad idea, Maddy. Thank you.

COLIN: Not at all, sir. I think I'll leave the bottle at your right hand, shall I? Is it sufficiently in the shade?

MADDY: Is he being sarcastic? I can never tell with him.

STEPHANIE: Well, he thinks he is. It's a cry for help really, isn't it, darling?

MADDY: So what *were* you talking about out here, you two?

TONY: Oh, everything, really. Gardening...

STEPHANIE: Aren't men wonderful?

TONY: Cars, a bit. What else, Colin?

STEPHANIE: You been relating, yeah? Reciporting?

TONY: What?

STEPHANIE: Yeah, you know, I thought you might have been embarking upon a caring and supportive relationship, sort of thing.

TONY: Sorry, this is going way over my head...

COLIN: What my wife is trying to say, in her tortured fashion – is that she's found out that both of us – you and I – are receiving some form of therapy. Okay? That's all. Not a big deal, is it? But she seems to think it's something deeply profound or noteworthy and not a little bit amusing, so good luck to her.

MADDY: No, we weren't laughing unkindly, were we, Steph?

COLIN: Oh no, it's never unkind! Perish the thought. It's just funny, that's all. And that's the main thing, isn't it? That our wives have a good giggle. I get a panic attack – ha ha ha; I wake up in the night – ha ha ha; I get on the train to go home, it's the wrong train – ha ha ha.

MADDY: Oh, you did that, didn't you, Tony?

TONY: Yes.

COLIN: Hilarious – let's all a have a laugh!

STEPHANIE: We're not laughing at the disease.

COLIN: Oh, it's a disease now, is it? You hear that, Tony? It's a disease now. We'd better keep clear of them; they'll catch it.

STEPHANIE: It's just the thought of you in a group – talking and – whatever it is you do. To total strangers.

COLIN: Yeah, I can see the humour of the situation. I must arrange for a video to be made. We can invite people round on Sunday afternoons to come and have a laugh. Anyway, they're not total strangers. As a matter of fact – I sometimes feel I know them better than my own family.

STEPHANIE: Well, that's why you're there, isn't it?

COLIN: Oh, that's why I'm there! Thank you very much, my dear – I've spent six months talking and wondering about why I'm there.

MADDY: I'm going to an acupuncturist, you know, because I've got this allergy to wheat.

COLIN: Every time I come away from there I feel like a new man. I get in the car and come back here and wallop! Straight back into the miserable wreck that I am.

STEPHANIE: Well, perhaps you ought to move in with them.

MADDY: Yes, that's not a bad idea, Colin...

COLIN: It's not a house, it's not a refuge. They all lead normal lives, like I do, with their families, poor sods.

STEPHANIE: You finished, Maddy?

MADDY: Oh yes, thank you, Steph; that was lovely.

COLIN: I had no intention of discussing this today. In fact, I believe it's been – totally counter-productive.

STEPHANIE: It has to come into the home sooner or later, Colin. Otherwise there's no point, is there? Are you going to eat that pie?

MADDY: Do you take your glasses off when you do it, Colin? 'When you do it!' (*Laughs.*) I didn't mean it like that at all! When you do your *therapy*.

COLIN: Do I what?

MADDY: No, I just wondered – when you're sitting in the circle and everything, and everyone's bearing their souls – do you take your glasses off? Because I can't imagine anyone bearing their souls wearing glasses.

COLIN: Well, if you *really* want to know – I do as a matter of fact.

MADDY: Ah, I was just curious, that's all.

COLIN: Oh, I see; it wasn't just gratuitous interest, then?

MADDY: No, no, I like to get a picture of it, you know.

COLIN: I know. Everyone wants a picture of everything these days. Honestly, the level of interest round here.

STEPHANIE: He really worries me when he takes his glasses off, actually...

MADDY: Does he? Yes, I was going to say.

STEPHANIE: You know what it's like when someone wears them all the time? And then suddenly he takes them off? It's quite disturbing actually. Because you've got these really deep-sunken eyes, haven't you, Colin? And you can't see a thing.

The women laugh again.

COLIN: Oh great – blindness now! It's not unkind, you know, not unkind. They're laughing about blindness. How about Ethiopia? Come on – lots of laughs in that.

STEPHANIE: We're not laughing at blindness, you twit.

COLIN: Oh, not laughing at blindness – excuse me, I thought I heard you can't see a thing and then… (*He imitates their laugh.*)

STEPHANIE: Oh, you don't understand humour.

COLIN: I know. I know I don't. That's exactly what my mother used to say to me.

STEPHANIE: If you could laugh at things more you wouldn't have to go, would you?

COLIN: I go because I have certain physical symptoms…

STEPHANIE: Oh, don't I know it!

COLIN: And not because I'm unable to laugh at blindness and AIDS victims. I don't find a great deal to laugh at in the world, to tell you the truth. I think we've made a proper mess of everything.

STEPHANIE: Who, us?

COLIN: No, the world.

STEPHANIE: Oh well, what d'you expect? Open that other bottle, will you please?

COLIN: Oh God, yes – got to keep Tony supplied here, haven't we?

TONY: Am I drinking too much?

MADDY: You are a bit, Tone.

COLIN: No, no, not at all – we've got another crate in the cellar, haven't we, Steph?

STEPHANIE: You've gone very quiet, Tony. You alright?

COLIN: I expect he's seeking a refuge in melancholy.

STEPHANIE: I didn't actually ask you, Colin.

COLIN: No, true enough.

STEPHANIE: I think he can speak for himself.

TONY: I didn't know you were going to a group.

COLIN: Me? Oh – yeah. (*Laughs.*) You know. There we go. Who wants it? You?

STEPHANIE: Try and exercise a little more charm if you're going to be the wine waiter, Colin.

COLIN: I've tried charm – where's it got me?

STEPHANIE: Thank you.

COLIN: You're welcome.

TONY: So how much is it costing you?

COLIN: I beg your pardon, Tony?

TONY: How much is your group costing you?

COLIN: Oh – about fifteen quid a go, I think.

TONY: Hm.

COLIN: Why – how much is it costing *you*? About ten quid a go, I expect.

TONY: Well, nothing actually. I was referred by my GP.

MADDY: I couldn't get my acupuncture like that. I tried.

COLIN: I see. How d'you manage that, then?

TONY: I don't know. I tried psychology; that didn't work, so I suppose he thought I needed it.

COLIN: Well, I didn't know you could get this sort of thing on the National Health.

STEPHANIE: Aren't they sweet when they talk together?

COLIN: I mean no one suggested I could apply for it. Muggins has to pay.

TONY: You can in Brent.

COLIN: Oh well, of course in Brent. (*Bitter laugh.*) You could probably get a series of Lesbian gym-mat meditations on the National Health in Brent.

MADDY: What's the latest one? One-legged, single-parent black steel band studies.

COLIN: Bloody typical, isn't it?

STEPHANIE: Now, now, Colin – don't be bitter.

COLIN: Well, it's completely ridiculous, isn't it? It's gone completely over the top. All of this comes out of your taxes, you know.

STEPHANIE: Oh come on, you're not paying that much.

COLIN: Yeah, but I'm paying, aren't I? I pay everything. Why can't someone, just once in a while, come along and say to me: here you are, let me pay for this. Let me take the load off your feet. I mean what do *you* pay?

STEPHANIE: I pay in ways you can't envisage.

COLIN: Do you? Huh!

MADDY: I think they're very useful, though – especially for men. So they can channel their natural aggression.

COLIN: IT'S NOTHING TO DO WITH AGGRESSION!

MADDY: Oh.

COLIN: Sorry.

STEPHANIE: Don't you think you're overdoing it, darling?

COLIN: Yeah I'm sorry but people will keep saying it's all to do with aggression. It isn't. I mean not all men are bloody Rambo or Hitler or something. It's supposed to make us understand, to perceive, to… (*He runs out of words.*)

STEPHANIE: Yes, but you're not there now, are you, darling? You do understand that, don't you? You're here, in this quiet garden, with your friends, in Ealing.

COLIN: Yeah, sorry. No need to sound like I'm a raving maniac. I mean, you know.

STEPHANIE: Why don't you eat something instead of smoking that nasty cigar?

COLIN: (*To TONY.*) What's the matter with you?

TONY: Nothing.

STEPHANIE: Don't snap so. 'What's the matter with you?' Tony's supposed to be a friend. It's not his fault he's getting free medicine.

COLIN: Yeah, I know but *I don't think to ask, you see.* Muggins.

STEPHANIE: Oh, don't let's go over all that again.

COLIN: I mean he just sits there drinking.

TONY: I *am* drinking too much, aren't I?

STEPHANIE: Of course you're not, Tony; we're very gratified it's to your taste, aren't we, Colin?

COLIN: Oh yeah, we're over the moon about that.

STEPHANIE: I like to see people enjoying things.

COLIN: And another thing...

STEPHANIE: Oh no.

COLIN: We do not sit in a circle shouting and baying at one another...

STEPHANIE: Alright.

COLIN: No, I just want to make this clear, because there are all kinds of popular misconceptions. We don't bay at one another; we talk; we listen; we relate. These are people who are in touch with their feelings. They might discuss anything – the variety is enormous. It might be a dream someone's had, a book someone's read, a film someone's seen – a topic of current import. The everyday phenomena of this phenomenal world.

MADDY: I can't bear hearing other people's dreams.

STEPHANIE: Oh, I know – they're so boring, aren't they?

MADDY: I mean I know they're interesting for *them*...

STEPHANIE: But not for others.

MADDY: No.

COLIN: Well, you obviously don't know how to read a dream, do you? You obviously don't know the basic symbols. If you dream about little furry animals, they're really your brothers and sisters and if you dream about a wardrobe it's your mother.

MADDY: A wardrobe?

STEPHANIE: I don't think I've ever dreamt about a wardrobe.

COLIN: It's just an example.

STEPHANIE: I think even if you know the wardrobe is really your mother it's still likely to be a pretty boring dream, isn't it? I mean there's not much a wardrobe can do, is there?

MADDY: Except have little baby wardrobes.

The women laugh.

COLIN: It's women who drive us mad and then they laugh at us when we seek help.

STEPHANIE: Now that is a very extreme remark, Colin.

COLIN: It was meant to be; it's true. You drive us bonkers. It's no wonder all these blokes are having analysis and doing therapy – it's women who've driven them there.

STEPHANIE: I'd like to see how you'd get on without us.

COLIN: Tony and I were having a perfectly calm and reasonable discussion out here and now you've – broken it up, broken it with your cynicism and your, your, complete unsensitivity.

STEPHANIE: It's 'insensitivity'.

COLIN throws wine in STEPHANIE's face.

STEPHANIE: (*Reacting to it.*) !!

MADDY: (*Reacting to it.*) !!

COLIN: (*Laughing.*) Sorry but I've always wanted to throw a glass of wine in someone's face...

MADDY: Are you alright, Steph?

STEPHANIE: (*Calmly.*) Yes, I'm alright.

MADDY: Think I've got a tissue here.

STEPHANIE: I'm alright thank you.

COLIN: Oh God, that felt so good!

STEPHANIE: It doesn't matter, Maddy; this is what I live with, that's all. If you live with this sort of person, this is what you have to put up with.

MADDY: It's soaked your blouse.

STEPHANIE: It feels quite refreshing actually.

COLIN: Oh look, I'm sorry, okay? Let's not make too much of it, come on. Give us a kiss, eh? (*He kisses her.*) That's it. It clears the air, it clears the air. It's all about relief, you see, and life moving on, as it must. I'll just refill the glass – and we start again.

MADDY: You're not going to do it again, are you?

COLIN: No, no, Maddy; I shall drink this one. (*He takes a deep breath.*) What a lovely day. Anyway – while we're on the subject – why do you go to your group, Tony?

TONY: Um…

COLIN: Because I've always thought you were a well-adjusted type, really, no problems or anything like that. Just getting on with life in unspectacular fashion. Not like me at all. (*Laughs.*)

TONY: Well, it's just to take the pressure off really.

MADDY: Yes, he's been under a lot of pressure at work, haven't you, Tony?

TONY: I've been under a lot of pressure at work.

MADDY: Yes.

COLIN: Yes, well…

TONY: But really, the thing that – precipitated it was the sensation that – I thought – I wanted to kill my wife.

COLIN: Oh.

TONY: Yes.

MADDY: It was then we thought we ought to consult the doctor.

COLIN: What did the doctor do?

MADDY: He prescribed valium.

COLIN: Not quite the thing, eh?

MADDY: Well, it wasn't really, no. It was worse actually. It meant he was calmer about it.

COLIN: Calmer about wanting to kill you?

MADDY: Mm.

COLIN: Did you want to kill anyone else, or just Maddy.

TONY: No, just her.

MADDY: (*Gamely.*) Don't know what I've done to deserve the honour, I must say!

COLIN: Well, it makes my symptoms sound quite routine, doesn't it, Steph?

STEPHANIE: Does it?

COLIN: What have you been doing to him, Maddy? Winding him up, have you?

MADDY: (*Upset.*) I don't know.

COLIN: Oh no! Sorry.

STEPHANIE: It's alright, Maddy.

COLIN: Now look what I've done.

MADDY: It wasn't you, Colin. It's just me being silly.

COLIN: (*Suddenly.*) What d'you want to kill her for?

STEPHANIE: Colin!

COLIN: No, I think he should tell us.

TONY: I know I don't *really* want to but – I don't know. It's the imagination, see. It won't let me be. I imagine myself doing it and it's almost as real as though I really am. Sometimes *as* real.

COLIN: But you haven't, have you? I mean here she is, in front of us in her nice frock.

MADDY: No, but the first time is the last time, isn't it?

COLIN: Yes, fair enough point, I suppose.

STEPHANIE: Here, have a drink – don't worry about it.

MADDY: I'm sorry.

COLIN: You ought to see a psychiatrist.

STEPHANIE: Oh, Colin.

COLIN: Well, of course he ought. A proper psychiatrist, not one of these groups. Because in groups, you know, they're reliable to egg you on.

STEPHANIE: Will you leave it, please?

COLIN: It's all this RD Laing stuff. If you feel like doing something crazy they say you should go ahead and do it, get it out of your system. Meanwhile the poor old victim's lying dead with her insides ripped out.

STEPHANIE: Look, I think we ought to drop the subject, actually.

TONY: I can be objective about it. I mean who in their right mind would want to kill Maddy?

COLIN: (*A beat.*) Well, no one.

TONY: She's completely inoffensive. She's the sort of person no one notices. And yet here I am – I want to kill her! It's completely outrageous.

COLIN: What weapon do you see yourself using?

STEPHANIE: That's enough, Colin.

COLIN: No, I was thinking – if we could sort of isolate the weapon – I mean is it a blunt instrument?

TONY: It's my bare hands. I want to take her neck in my bare hands and squeeze and squeeze until I can feel the life – ebbing away.

MADDY: That's just the way he is.

STEPHANIE: Does he watch a lot of television, yeah?

COLIN: I think he ought to call the Samaritans.

STEPHANIE: What about Maddy?

COLIN: Well, I think she ought to call them too. Phoo, it's a bit heavy, isn't it, Tony?

TONY: I had it earlier on actually. When I heard you laughing in there. I wanted to go in there and – I wanted to end that tinkling, chiming laugh, just put an end to it. That must have been around the time you were giving me those funny looks, Colin.

STEPHANIE: I thought you were talking about gardening.

COLIN: We were.

MADDY: Am I living with a monster, Steph? Tell me – am I?

STEPHANIE: Well, I think there are grounds for concern, Maddy, yes.

COLIN: Grounds for concern? He ought to be locked up. He ought to be put in a padded cell. No disrespect, old chap but – phoo! Bit heavy, isn't it?

TONY: What makes you think you're any different?

COLIN: Me? Well, of course I'm different!

TONY: Huh!

COLIN: What – kill Steph? But I love her!

TONY: You just threw a glass of wine in her face.

COLIN: Yeah, well that's normal, isn't it? That's family life, isn't it, Steph?

STEPHANIE: It does seem to be, yes.

COLIN: Kill my wife? I never wanted to kill anyone. I wouldn't even know where to start.

TONY: It's easy.

COLIN: You're just trying to excuse yourself by saying it's what everyone wants to do. But it's a trick; you're psychotic. Maddy? You're staying here with us until further notice.

MADDY: But what about the kids?

COLIN: It's alright – he doesn't want to kill them. You don't, do you?

TONY: I'm alright most of the time.

COLIN: Well, that's what makes it all the more disturbing, isn't it? Sitting out here making small-talk with me about trellises and Russian vine and really you're having these fantasies about strangling your wife.

MADDY: He was alright when I married him.

TONY: What do you know?

MADDY: Oh! How long has this been going on?

TONY: Always.

COLIN: Always? But you haven't 'always' been married. I mean have you? You haven't always wanted to kill Maddy because you haven't always been married to her. You see that, don't you?

TONY: Yes, I see that.

COLIN: You see, you can reason with him.

STEPHANIE: They're always logical.

COLIN: Yes, I suppose that's true. Eh, what's the matter?

MADDY: Aah! That's the way he looks when he...

STEPHANIE: Grab hold of him, Colin...

COLIN: Come on, Tony, don't be a fool. Let's just talk ab...

TONY: (*Making strange werewolf-type noises.*) Kill you... kill you...

MADDY: (*Screaming.*) Sorry, I'd better... (*She rushes off.*)

STEPHANIE: Maddy!

TONY: It's alright, Maddy – come back! It's alright now.

STEPHANIE: You stay with him.

COLIN: Me?

STEPHANIE: Stay with him; I'll see to Maddy.

COLIN: Oh right. Okay, yeah. If you want to give her one of my pills, they're in the...

STEPHANIE: (*Some way off by now.*) I know. You stay there. (*She goes.*)

Pause.

COLIN: Steph'll see to her.

TONY: Oh dear.

COLIN: No, no.

TONY: I was afraid something like this might happen.

COLIN: Well, you know, it happens, doesn't it? You can't predict these things. Hm. (*Pause.*) Well! (*Pause while he lights his cigar.*) The old cigar's gone out. (*Laughs nervously.*) What you going to have to drink, Tony?

TONY: I'll stay with the wine, I think.

COLIN: Good idea. Well! Gone quiet all of a sudden, eh? Yes, sir. It's not the first of April, is it?

TONY: How d'you mean?

COLIN: Well, I mean you wouldn't be having us on, would you? It wouldn't be a sort of practical joke.

TONY: It must seem that way. I must seem like an absolute lunatic.

COLIN: Well no, I mean it's…

TONY: It wouldn't be a joke in good taste, would it?

COLIN: No, it wouldn't. Besides. I don't think Maddy could turn it on like that, quite frankly. She was clearly in a state of distress.

TONY: Oh yes, they're very quick to get into a state.

COLIN: Mm, right, of course. It just came out of the blue, then, that's all?

TONY: I'm sorry.

COLIN: No, no, no need to apologise. Enough said, eh?

TONY: Yeah.

COLIN: We all spoke out of turn rather. It's gone quiet – I hope they're alright.

TONY: Oh, *they'll* be alright.

COLIN: It's been quite an interesting afternoon in a way.

TONY: (*In a curious new voice.*) Beats watching the cricket.

COLIN: Oh I say, yeah, have you been watching it?

TONY: Yes I have.

COLIN: I mean, they're just got no idea, have they?

TONY: None whatsoever.

COLIN: I mean how they think they can go into a five day test match with only four front-line bowlers...

TONY: Two of whose fitness is under serious question.

COLIN: Exactly. I mean Dilley has never been a hundred per cent.

TONY: And now Foster's broken down.

COLIN: But even fit they're not going to bowl out a side like the West Indies, are they?

TONY: Of course they're not.

COLIN: No way are they going to win with a side like that.

TONY: And they've got to win this one because they're already four down.

COLIN: That's right.

TONY: Mind you...

COLIN: Yeah.

TONY: ...I don't like the way the West Indians play the game.

COLIN: Oh no.

TONY: All this short-pitched bowling: it's outside the spirit of the game.

COLIN: Of course it is. I mean anyone can win like that.

TONY: They're definitely bowling at the man.

COLIN: Those balls should be called wides.

TONY: They should be but the umpires are scared of them. I know for a fact – I know somebody who knows Emburey.

COLIN: Really? And he said that?

TONY: Course it would be different if we picked some batsmen who could hook the ball.

COLIN: Absolutely; the art of hooking is dead.

TONY: It is dead. They don't get into the position, these modern batsmen.

COLIN: I think their bats are too heavy.

TONY: I think they're scared.

COLIN: I think some of them are.

TONY: Scared of getting out and missing the next game.

COLIN: Yeah well, it's all money, isn't it?

TONY: And I don't like that new all-rounder they've chosen. No way can he ever be a replacement for Botham.

COLIN: Well, I know but who could be?

TONY: They could try Wells of Sussex.

COLIN: Possible.

TONY: I mean De Freitas is alright...

COLIN: Very promising.

TONY: But no way is he a batsman.

COLIN: Certainly not a Botham.

TONY: Who is?

COLIN: It's all to do with confidence, how you feel about yourself.

TONY: Yes.

They have come to a stop.

COLIN: Your cigar gone out, Tony?

TONY looks at him as though he doesn't understand.

– Your cigar. It's out.

TONY looks at it.

– Here, let me give you a light. Oh, sorry… A sudden freakish gust of wind. Here you are – I'll cup my hands around it. You just draw.

COLIN helps him to get his cigar going. TONY seems un-coordinated, all of a sudden, utterly at sea with the idea of the cigar. It takes a long time. Meanwhile, from the house, the women are heard laughing.

Lights slowly down.

End of Act One.

ACT TWO

Another garden. This time, the day is not so sunny, but there are moments of sunshine sometimes noted in the text. At these moments the characters respond – they bask in it etc. However, this is not the garden of an ordinary house; it is the grounds of an asylum somewhere in North London. At the start we see TONY slumped in a chair, with tea things spread out. He is wearing some kind of distinctive uniform, marking him as an inmate – although his demeanour suggests straightaway that there is something wrong. Also, MADDY is next to him, clipping his fingernails. He gives his hand over to her during this operation as though not realising what's going on. He is well out of it and looks drugged-up.

MADDY expects nothing of him; she doesn't really expect him to speak. But this doesn't stop her addressing him, and when she does so she adopts a strange voice, as though she's talking to a small child – scolding and patronising at the same time.

STEPHANIE is there too.

There are signs of other inmates, especially the occasional sound of male laughter, off. COLIN is making the others laugh.

MADDY: I never thought I'd be able to do this for somebody else but you can get used to anything, can't you?

STEPHANIE looks at the fingers. She says nothing.

(*To TONY.*) Alright? You've been chewing these, haven't you? Hm? How come you always choose this one and not that one? Hm? Taste nicer, does it? Hm? I don't know. They don't half leave them unattended, though, don't you think?

STEPHANIE: Hm.

MADDY: All those wandering about down by the fence when we came in – I don't think that's right; it must put the motorists off. And it's not very nice for the children, is it?

STEPHANIE: I think they were trustees.

MADDY: Well, I don't know. They can't be right or they wouldn't be here, would they? (*To TONY.*) Hold still! I expect it takes them time to lose that, you know – that funny look. They can't let them out until people can accept them back into the community, can they? I mean, it's all well and good, but I wouldn't want to let a room to one of them. I can quite understand people not... (*She sniffs.*) I believe in giving people a fair chance but fair's fair, isn't it?

STEPHANIE: Yes, they're very hard to take.

MADDY: They are. The woman who ran our local off-license, she took one on – I don't know what he was – but she said she'd give him a chance, you know. The moment her back was turned he murdered her. She had her head all stoved-in. It said on the news, they didn't know it was possible to actually be able to hit someone that hard. Because you see they're stronger. Oh – that was nice – bit of sunlight... Oh, it's gone. Still it's warm; that's the main thing. (*To TONY.*) Nice to have your tea out in the garden, isn't it? Every day. They bring it out here for you? His hands are boiling.

STEPHANIE: Yeah well, they generate a lot of heat. They're like nuclear reactors.

MADDY: Mm.

STEPHANIE: Not that they're going to *blow* or anything. (*To TONY.*) Are you?

MADDY: Poor devils.

STEPHANIE: Well, I feel a lot more sorry for those stuck inside...

MADDY: Oh yes!

STEPHANIE: Did you see them?

MADDY: Yes, I did. I'm sorry, I felt sick.

STEPHANIE: With a toilet in their wheelchairs…

MADDY: No, sorry, I definitely can't take that actually.

STEPHANIE: It's so humiliating for the men. You have to remind yourself; they were the breadwinners, weren't they?

MADDY: Now they don't win anything. They're just vegetables really. I don't know how those nurses cope, I really don't. I mean could you do that job?

STEPHANIE: No.

MADDY: It would be the very last thing for me; I know it sounds selfish, but… I mean it's not so bad if they're just ill – that's natural, but when there's the mental thing as well, it's sort of unpleasant, isn't it? When they reach that stage.

STEPHANIE: Well, I know I couldn't do it.

MADDY: It sounds an awful thing to say but, well, you can quite understand why some countries, you know, have them put down. Because they're not going to play any serious function in society any more, are they? I don't mean like Hitler – that's definitely going too far, but… I just think, when it's for their own good, sort of thing.

STEPHANIE: Well, I think they should just pay the nurses what they ask for.

MADDY: Oh so do I. Mind you, it is vocation for them; it wouldn't be the same if they were paid vast amounts. Like I think in America, I don't think there's a sort of human element with the nurses and the hospitals there.

STEPHANIE: Well, they seem very nice.

MADDY: Oh yes. Very cheerful. That black one was nice. She said she'd bring our tea out for us.

STEPHANIE: I suppose the only way they can stand it is by cutting off.

MADDY: Yes.

They sit vacantly for a moment. The sun passes between the clouds again. They both narrow their eyes and sway slightly.

(*To TONY.*) See, I brought you some ginger cake! He used to love ginger cake. He always used to love anything with a bit of a spicy taste, you know. We'll all have a bit, shall we, Steph?

STEPHANIE: Alright.

They start eating the cake. TONY is given a piece. He sits holding it like a baby. He watches them eating theirs.

MADDY: Where's Colin got to?

STEPHANIE: Oh he's gone wandering off over there.

MADDY: He's a real rover, your husband, isn't he?

STEPHANIE: Oh yes. I don't think he likes to see Tony, you know.

MADDY: (*Eating.*) No. (*To TONY.*) Well none of us do, do we? That's why we're going to have to get you better, isn't it? Yes! You should see the vine now. Right up over the wall, it is. I told them next door they were welcome to train it over if they wanted to. But that dog keeps coming over still, I'm afraid. You remember we went and bought the trellis to keep it out? Well, unfortunately the dog's grown but the trellis hasn't – so it keeps jumping over. I don't know if he hears me or not but

I think it's a good idea to maintain a flow of pleasant banter.

STEPHANIE: Oh he can hear you, Maddy.

MADDY: D'you think so?

STEPHANIE: Oh yes. He sort of registers with his eyes. It's hard to explain.

MADDY: He probably relates to the familiarity.

STEPHANIE: Well it's like a cat, isn't it? My cat'll sit there while I'm talking and I think she's paying no attention but I look at her tail and I see it's waving from side to side. 'Cos she's listening.

MADDY: I thought that was when they were angry.

STEPHANIE: Well that's when they *really* wave it. Oh no, that's quite different. No, this is just a sort of nice sort of gentle wafting.

MADDIE: Mm.

They look at TONY.

Aren't you going to eat your cake? It's nice! Look, we're eating! Mm!

STEPHANIE: He's watching you, Maddy.

MADDY: Eat it while he's looking.

They demonstrate eating the cake.

– Mm! Isn't this ginger cake nice, Stephanie?

He puts it to his lips and starts eating it slowly.

STEPHANIE: I wish they could treat them without so many drugs, though.

MADDY: Yeah. But then you've got to consider – what would they be like without them?

STEPHANIE: Oh yes, I know…

MADDY: You've got to think of that.

STEPHANIE: Oh yes, well I don't know what the answer is.

MADDY: Because you can't – *unleash...* (*She stops.*)

STEPHANIE: No. It's nice, this cake. Where d'you get it?

MADDY: Marks.

STEPHANIE: Oh yes, I thought so – you can't beat Marks.

MADDY: I don't mind paying that little bit extra, Steph.

STEPHANIE: Well, it's not paying extra if it's benefiting you in quality.

MADDY: This is it.

STEPHANIE: I don't think people mind paying more if they know they're getting good quality. I mean I think that's why Labour lost the last election.

MADDY: Well, you see the women queuing up in Tesco's and they're enormous – you know, great blubbery white arms and cheeks all out here – and you look at what they've got in their trolleys: sliced white bread, chips, everything tinned, and it's no surprise, is it?

Noises off: COLIN and men laughing.

STEPHANIE: Tsk. Trust him; he always falls in with people.

MADDY: He's cheerful wherever he goes, isn't he? It's a talent of sorts.

STEPHANIE: He's making them laugh, anyway.

MADDY: It's a very precious commodity, the gift of laughter. There's no money in the world can buy that, Stephanie. (*To TONY.*) Look at Colin, making them all laugh.

More laughter.

STEPHANIE: I hope he's not getting them too worked up.

MADDY: (*To TONY.*) Here, let me take this off you, love.

She takes the cake away from TONY, as though from a baby. He watches it all the way back to the plate.

STEPHANIE: He learned some horrible stories when he was working at Plessey's, you know. I don't know what it was about that firm, but he seemed to pick up a new story every day there. Course, he'd have to come straight back and tell it to me. 'Listen to this one, Steph.'

MADDY: Like kids sometimes, aren't they?

STEPHANIE: He ended up with an inexhaustible supply. Except I was exhausted.

MADDY: He's a very tiring man, Steph.

STEPHANIE: (*Looking off.*) I think they're just responding to the sound of his voice. He could be reading the phone book and they'd laugh.

More laughter, off. By now TONY is crying.

MADDY: Oh! What's the matter...? What's the matter? What is it? Oh God!

STEPHANIE: It's because they keep laughing. I knew it would go wrong... Colin! Stop that! Stop it!

Actually TONY is crying because of the cake.

MADDY: (*To TONY.*) He's only telling the others a joke! You don't mind if they have a laugh, do you? You don't begrudge them that, do you? Hm?

STEPHANIE: Come over here! Come on!

MADDY: (*To TONY.*) What d'you want, your cake back? Here.

She thrusts the cake back at him. He clutches it and stops crying. But the women still don't see the connection.

– My mother always used to say 'Laughter ends in tears.'

STEPHANIE: Yes, my gran said that.

MADDY: And it's true; it does.

STEPHANIE: Yes. It's a terrible shame for him, Maddy.

MADDY: It's hard to believe somehow, isn't it? You see he's alright now. (*To TONY.*) They weren't laughing at you! Did you think they were laughing at you? They've got far better things to be laughing about. (*To STEPHANIE.*) You've got no idea what passes through their heads, have you?

STEPHANIE: I'd hate to see a film of it.

MADDY: (*Shivers.*) Oooh! What a thought!

STEPHANIE: I expect they'll be able to do that one day. They won't be able to cure it, but they will be able to film it.

MADDY: Is it summer or what?

STEPHANIE: It's nice when the sun's out.

MADDY: I know but it's such a long time waiting.

STEPHANIE: It'll be alright when that big cloud shifts. Oh, look at him with that coat on… COLIN! Come on! He does it to spite me.

MADDY: I don't think he does, Steph.

STEPHANIE: Oh, I know him.

MADDY: I suppose I should have talked to him more. That's what they always say, isn't it? Talk it over and get it out in the open, sort of thing? The trouble is, he's always been a bit cleverer than me. My mother always

used to say 'Never marry 'em cleverer than yourself.'
A bit difficult in my case. I mean I'd never have got
married, would I?

STEPHANIE: Don't be silly.

MADDY: He's always used words I don't understand.
I'd look them up and everything, but then I'd go and
forget them. Whereas he – he'd look them up and
straightaway he'd be – peppering his conversation with
them. He would, he'd pepper it. And I'd stop and say
'Eh, that's the word you didn't know yesterday and had
to look up!' The looks he used to give me. Especially
when it was somebody he was out to impress. Used to
embarrass him something dreadful. (*She laughs.*) But it is
a bit of a cheat, that, isn't it? Pretending you've always
talked like that when you've only just learned what the
word means.

STEPHANIE: Oh, I suppose so.

MADDY: You don't have to agree with me.

STEPHANIE: No, it's just that men don't like to be teased.

MADDY: (*Indignant.*) Well, I know but… I never did it in
a nasty way.

STEPHANIE: No.

MADDY: I mean, did it sound nasty to you, the way
I described it?

STEPHANIE: No, no.

MADDY: Because I mean, you've got to keep your feet on
the ground, haven't you? Everyone has.

STEPHANIE: Oh yes.

MADDY: It's all part of being married.

STEPHANIE: (*Smiling.*) Yes.

MADDY: No, I never teased him as such. (*To TONY.*) You're not eating that, are you? You just want to hold onto it like a baby, don't you? Hm? We shall have to bring you a little blanket or something next time, shan't we?

STEPHANIE: Let him hold it; he's sucking it.

MADDY: Yeah I know but… (*Looking at him as though at a problematic painting.*) It's all going down his… Tsk! Look at the state of you though, Tony. I mean, you're supposed to *have* your faculties. The laundry bills must be enormous.

COLIN comes bounding on. He's wearing a buttoned-up coat. He speaks in a rush.

COLIN: Eh, there are some really interesting boys over there…

STEPHANIE: What are you doing, getting everyone worked up?

COLIN: Alright, Tone?

He ruffles TONY's hair.

STEPHANIE: Don't do that!

MADDY: …I don't think he feels it, Steph…

COLIN: …One of them, he said, he said the sister asked him if he'd crapped in his pants.

STEPHANIE: I beg your pardon?

MADDY: (*Starting again.*) One of them said, he said the sister asked him if he'd crapped in his pants.

STEPHANIE: That's what I thought you said.

MADDY: Thank you very much, Colin.

COLIN: He said, 'No, I haven't. I haven't crapped in my pants.' He resented the suggestion not a little. The sister said 'Well, there's a terrific smell coming from you; are you sure you haven't crapped your pants?' He was getting a bit, you know, indignant by now, so he said 'Look, I haven't crapped my pants – how about leaving me alone?' So the sister went away, but there was still complaints about Percy. That's his name, Percy. Still complaints about him stinking. So the sister comes back, this time with a couple of heavies, male nurses – and they go up to him and they pull down his trousers. And there it is: all these turds, all piled up, steaming ones, congealed ones, the lot – and stinking to high heaven. 'There you are,' she says, 'I knew you'd crapped yourself!' So he says, 'Oh, I thought you meant *today!*'

MADDY: Euch – do you mind!

TONY has laughed at this story.

– Sorry, I think that's really pathetic. It's just schoolboy, isn't it?

STEPHANIE: Someone thinks it's funny.

COLIN: Good, eh Tone?

He ruffles TONY's hair again.

STEPHANIE: Don't do that. It's not true, is it?

COLIN: Hm?

STEPHANIE: That horrible story – it's not true, is it?

COLIN: True? Well, ah, how do you mean?

STEPHANIE: Well, did it really happen?

COLIN: The story's true; I don't know if it really happened or not.

STEPHANIE: Well, that's rather a contradiction, isn't it? How can a story be true if the incident it refers to never took place?

COLIN: Well, it's true... It's – truthful. It was true at the time.

He laughs weakly. He has taken off his coat by now, and we see that he too is an inmate. All the zest goes out of him. He transforms. He slumps in his chair. He starts to weep.

STEPHANIE: Oh God, I told you you shouldn't have gone over there. You've always got to start showing off.

MADDY: I expect he was excited because...

STEPHANIE: No, he's always like this. I don't know why you couldn't have stayed with us.

COLIN has set TONY off crying too.

MADDY: Oh no...

STEPHANIE: Look what you've done to Tony; he was perfectly alright before you came upsetting him.

The two men check on one another and before long they stop crying and start laughing instead.

MADDY: Oh, laughing now – you don't know where you are with them, do you?

COLIN ruffles TONY's hair.

STEPHANIE: Don't *do* that.

MADDY: I suppose this is what they call a violent mood-swing.

STEPHANIE: It's exactly like having a hyper-active child...

MADDY: Oh, I know someone who's got one of those. She says she can never...

COLIN: (*Suddenly.*) Oh great! Ginger cake!

He crams it into his mouth. They sit and watch him.

STEPHANIE: We could charge for this, Maddy. It's better than the chimps' tea party.

But they don't laugh. Silence as they watch COLIN devour most of the cake. They don't try to restrain him. The sun comes out for a moment. STEPHANIE puts her head back and basks in it. While it lasts.

COLIN: (*At last.*) Very nice. What's for tea?

STEPHANIE: Oh dear – that ancient joke.

COLIN and TONY laugh.

MADDY: Sorry, what did he say?

STEPHANIE: Maddy brought that for Tony, you know.

COLIN: Yeah, I guessed.

STEPHANIE: Well, it wasn't very friendly to go and eat it, was it?

COLIN: Tony's off his scoff.

MADDY: Well, he must eat sometimes, mustn't he?

COLIN: Yeah, he eats sometimes. You can see, if you want.

STEPHANIE: Rather difficult if you go and bolt the lot, isn't it?

MADDY: I'm not here at meal-times, am I?

COLIN: No, you're not.

MADDY: The food alright, is it?

COLIN: Pardon?

MADDY: I say, is the…

COLIN: What's the matter with your voice?

MADDY: There's nothing the matter with my voice. At least I speak.

COLIN: Oh yes, you do speak. Birds would speak if they could. I can hear them, longing to. The food? Don't ask me about the food. But since you ask – it's okay, but it makes you hungry.

MADDY: The food makes you hungry? Well...

COLIN: Yeah, it's the taste. It's the taste that – gives it the taste. I mean it's a *taster*. The taste of the taste – *tastes* like the taste of – something or other.

MADDY: Well, we're lucky I brought some jam-tarts here as well...

COLIN: Great! Hand 'em over!

He leaps on her bag.

STEPHANIE: Colin! Stop it!

COLIN: It's alright, I'm only joking.

STEPHANIE: Well, we don't know that, do we?

COLIN: I can just sit and look at them; I don't have to eat them. There's a man in Cuba who can reach orgasm – he can *come* – just by sitting there. No hands, no tricks, just mind. He does it on the stage.

MADDY: We're hearing a lot today, aren't we?

COLIN: (*Cockney.*) Yeah, it's heducition, ennit?

STEPHANIE: You'd better watch your weight while you're in here; don't want you coming out like a roly-poly.

COLIN: If I'm a jam one at least I can eat myself.

STEPHANIE: (*She surprises herself by laughing.*) He does say some funny things sometimes.

COLIN: Who does?

MADDY: Are you getting enough exercise in here, are you?

COLIN: Is she talking to me in that voice again?

STEPHANIE: Don't be rude.

MADDY: It's your fault; you're laughing at him all the time.

STEPHANIE: No, it's just that he takes you by surprise, some of things he comes out with.

COLIN: Exercise – my God. They chase us round the dorms with bullwhips every night. They use us instead of toilet-brushes. They use us for target-practice. That's why I like to keep on the move. You can't hit a – that's why he sits still. He likes being hit. Lesson one: paranoiacs are scared people because they expect everyone to do to them what they want to do to everyone else. Unto everyone else, as the Bible would say. Been reading the Bible. Good bits in it, some far-fetched bits. Better than the film. The film shirked the sado-masochism. Read the Song of Solomon – fucking hell, though; talk about horny. He had it alright, didn't he? I mean if it's true. You'd probably want to be sure it was true, wouldn't you? No, but no wonder he knew a lot, that randy old bastard Solomon. If everyone was screwing all the time, you'd see the national IQ go soaring. It would go right off the graph. Ought to start a self-help scheme – based on bedroom activities. From bedroom to boardroom in one easy lesson, knock those fucking Japs right out of the window, 'cos they lack stamina, I know that for a fact. What was I talking about?

MADDY: That's a good question.

COLIN: I started off on something and…

MADDY: It's no good trying to answer him, is it?

COLIN: (*To TONY.*) What was I talking about?

MADDY: (*To STEPHANIE.*) Don't mention exercise again.

COLIN: Ah, exercise, yes!

But he has nothing more to say. He slumps.

MADDY: Oh. That seems to be it.

COLIN: Tea's cold. How can we – with cold tea? I mean hot drinks, I mean it's basic that, isn't it? Even in hot countries. You have a hot drink and the body cools down and the tea cools. Miners drink it cold in the pit.

MADDY: (*Shakes her head.*) Phoo!

STEPHANIE: What's all this bunting and fairy-lights up for?

COLIN: What? Oh, disco, isn't it? Disco.

STEPHANIE: Disco, here?

COLIN: Yeah, disco here. Discowere.

MADDY: I expect they have it for nurses. And for the better ones, you know.

COLIN: If they're better they're not in here. Or you mean the better nurses?

STEPHANIE: Well, I expect it does them good to let their hair down once in a while.

MADDY: I suppose it's alright for some of them, so long as they don't get to expect it, you know.

She looks at COLIN; he smiles at her.

– Remember that holiday we went on to Majorca? And we learned that Saturday Night Fever routine, d'you remember?

STEPHANIE: We were quite good at it.

MADDY: We were.

COLIN: I was.

STEPHANIE: Oh yes, of course *you* were.

COLIN: I still do it. In the bathroom. They seem to think it's good for me. So long as I don't get to expect it, you know. Long as I keep my place. They like watching me. I'm unashamed.

MADDY: John Travolta, are you, in the privacy of your own bathroom?

COLIN: Yeah, in the privacy of my own… In the privacy of my own. Good-looking man.

MADDY: Who, John Travolta? Got over that stage a long time ago.

COLIN: That's good.

Short pause. Then COLIN lunges forward and ruffles TONY's hair again.

STEPHANIE: Colin? Do you mind me saying, love? If you ruffle Tony's hair – I'm sure it's nice for him and everything but, why don't you try doing it a bit more gently? Because at the moment I think it might be upsetting him.

COLIN looks at her as though not understanding.

COLIN: Oh. Sorry. (*To TONY.*) Sorry. Yes, quite right actually. Got to learn about stuff like that, haven't I?

MADDY: Oh, I don't suppose it matters…

COLIN: No, it does; it does matter. I've got to learn. We've all got to learn. People's hair is…well, sometimes it's all they've got, isn't it? (*Looks at STEPHANIE.*) My love. My darling. With your legs and your neck and your hair, the way it…the way you… I adore you. Playing tennis. Standing up against the sink, the way you – lean forward against the sink. In that striped apron. Our

holiday in – Madeira. That walk we went on with the
Bougain... Bougain... Bougain...

STEPHANIE: Bougainvillaea.

Pause.

The sun comes out. STEPHANIE basks in it.

COLIN: Over the balconies, the high walls. I'd kiss you,
I would. I'd put you in a book, a secret book, a diary,
so when I die you'd see how much I loved you, adored
you, how much I thought the things I never said, no
one ever says. My secret life, all of it, the adorableness
of my life with you, on that walk, I can see the imprint of
your shoe, now, in the sunshine overlooking the sea at
Madeira.

Pause.

MADDY: Well! It's supposed to be nice in Madeira. I
know a couple who went there.

STEPHANIE: We went there.

MADDY: No, but another couple. They went in the winter.
They had ever such a good time. They said it wasn't
such a good place to go if you wanted discos and all
that, and they said it did get cold at nights, But you can't
have everything, can you? (*To TONY.*) Your tax rebate
came through. You remember? You were worried they'd
miscalculated it? Well, it came through. Three hundred
and twenty pounds fifty it was. Plus your sickness
benefit, it works out a tidy sum. We'll be able to have
a nice little holiday on that when you come out. If it's
winter we could go to Florida. Remember you said you
wanted to go to Florida? They say there's a lot of crime
in Florida – it spoils everything, crime, doesn't it?

She notices that TONY is looking fixedly at her.

Alright? Did you want to say something?

COLIN: You should have heard him this morning.

MADDY: I should? Why, what did he say?

COLIN: It wasn't so much what he *said*... Sorry, you're talking about what he said in words, aren't you?

MADDY: Well, what else?

COLIN: He gave a very good account of himself. He's always like that after psychotherapy.

MADDY: (*To TONY.*) Did you have a good session with the doctor then?

COLIN: He's not a doctor; he's a psychotherapist.

MADDY: It's the same thing.

COLIN: He wears a buttonhole. We all like that. He's got a packet of Kleenex on his desk and a mug with a blue hippopotamus on it. He's just trying to catch us out. Only doing his job, I suppose. It's okay with him if you sit there in silence for an hour.

MADDY: I don't expect you do that, Colin.

COLIN: No, I don't.

MADDY: (*To TONY.*) You talk to him, do you?

COLIN: God yes, he doesn't get a word in.

STEPHANIE: (*Laughing.*) She was talking to Tony.

COLIN: Sorry. Shit.

MADDY: We know *you* talk, Colin.

COLIN: Oh, he talks too. You should hear him.

MADDY: I'd like to very much.

COLIN: He'd talk the hind leg off a...

MADDY: So what do you say then? Hm? Hm? Colin says you talk all the time, what do you say? Hm?

COLIN: Well, perhaps not 'all the time.'

MADDY: What do you talk to the doctor about? Hm? Hm? If you can talk then you can talk now, can't you? Hm? Hm?

She strokes his head experimentally at first. Then again, with more conviction.

– I'm interested, aren't I? Because I want to help you. There are some things I want to seriously discuss with you. We want to build you up and get you moving. We all miss you; Toby and Chloe; they miss you; they ask after their dad. They say 'When's Dad coming home?'

COLIN: (*Laughing.*) That's nice, isn't it? Just like kids that, isn't it? Where's my tea? What's on telly? When's Dad coming home?

He ruffles TONY's hair. MADDY is irritated but it makes TONY laugh.

– See, he's laughing now.

MADDY: Well, you certainly seem to possess the necessary talent to make him respond, Colin.

COLIN: It's 'cos I'm a fucking nutcase myself.

MADDY: No, it's very good. I only wish I had it. I've lived with him for ten years and he only looks at me as he wants to... (*To STEPHANIE.*) I must find out what he says. They'll tell me if I ask, won't they?

COLIN: They might, but it's not the same; you've got to be there.

MADDY: Yes well, I'm *not* there, am I?

STEPHANIE: I should think they'll tell you.

MADDY: I've got to see them anyway.

COLIN: They'll show you a film of it, if you ask. Didn't you know? They film us. At work and play. And at defecation. Little bug-eyed cameras. Bug-eyed people, bug-eyed telly. You know the plug in the sink? That's a camera. It always has been. It films you while you vomit. They've got to because they can tell a lot from vomit, you know. It's not just old carrot and shepherd's pie to them; it's evidence. It's material. There's a whole puke read-out available; the government knows all about it. They're probably filming us now, hoping we'll all start spewing up.

MADDY: Vivid imagination he's got anyway.

COLIN: Yeah, it's got a lot sharper since I came in here.

MADDY: Has it? That's good, isn't it?

COLIN: They film you in Amsterdam, in the Van Gogh Museum, in case you... (*He stops.*) Van Gogh. Bloody hell! (*He holds his head.*) Oh! Van *Gogh!* (*He starts to cry again.*)

MADDY: Oh dear. He gets upset so easily.

STEPHANIE: He relates everything... I don't know. He can't keep up with his thoughts. It's terrible, but I think I'm beginning to understand it.

COLIN: Explain it to me.

He has set TONY off too.

MADDY: See? Now Tony. God, what are we going to do, Steph? I've got to go and talk to them; I can't take any more of this.

She doesn't move.

– Perhaps we'd better go home.

COLIN: You don't go home! You don't leave here...

MADDY: ...Excuse me, do you mind? I shall do what I
like...

COLIN: (*Continuing.*) ...Until the appointed – you fulfil
your role; you stay your time, you do the necessary,
and then perhaps you do a little extra. Here and in
Hendon and in England and in life, forever and forever.
Afterwards, you're on your own. Then it's a terrible,
terrible different matter. But now you're here. With
the ginger cakes and the jam tarts. The tarts have to be
eaten. In your sight. The innocent words, the silences,
the jam tarts. Get it? They've got lots of games in the
common room. Monopoly and all that. I always win.
Afterwards there will be dancing. Indoors if wet. Is
everybody happy?

TONY: You bet your life we are!

He and COLIN laugh.

MADDY: Ah, so that's how it's done. Do it again, Colin.

COLIN: Do what?

MADDY: What you just did.

COLIN: What was that?

MADDY: When he responded to you just now.

COLIN: Again?

MADDY: Yes, go on.

COLIN: God, no one's ever asked me to say things *again.*

MADDY: Well, I am. Go on.

COLIN: Well, I've got to think now. When he laughed,
you mean?

MADDY: Yes – he responded.

COLIN: Right. What was that? (*Thinks.*) Percy, wasn't it? Yes. The sister says to him 'Hey, have you crapped your pants…?'

MADDY: No, not that – that was ages ago…

COLIN: I thought you meant the story…

MADDY: No… Oh, can't you get him to do it, Steph?

STEPHANIE: (*Quietly.*) 'Is everybody happy?'

COLIN: (*Loudly.*) You bet your life we are!

MADDY: Oh! *He's* meant to do it, not you.

COLIN: Oh.

Silence.

MADDY: (*To TONY.*) Is everybody happy?

Silence.

Is everybody happy?

COLIN: (*Puzzled.*) You bet your life we are? Is it?

MADDY: Oh forget it; it doesn't matter.

COLIN: Sorry, are you asking me, Maddy?

MADDY: Crap.

STEPHANIE: It's alright, forget it now.

COLIN: Sorry, have I, um…?

STEPHANIE: It's alright.

MADDY: He was doing that deliberately, wasn't he? I mean you can tell, can't you?

COLIN: I don't know if you can 'tell'. Sometimes I think I'm worse that I am, you know? For instance, they gave me the library duties. The mobile library came round; I unloaded it, but instead of putting the books in the common room, I put them in the kitchen. Along with

all the pots and pans. I even put one book in the fridge.
Because it was called Ice Station Zebra. Daft, isn't it?
But it felt right at the time. It felt right but looking back
I can't really say it's the act of a sane man. Not
really. It's more than eccentric. It's not really the
sort of behaviour calculated to get you back into the
community, is it? And that's the idea, I know. To get out
there, into the community, where everything is white
and sane and even. Deep and crisp and even. Where
Christmas comes once a year, and in that order. You
can't release a git who goes and puts the library books
in the fridge, can you?
I can see that. But my point is, it's not hurting anybody,
is it? Not really. It doesn't mean that I want to go and
put you in the fridge. Does it? Or does it? I mean, is
this the way they think? Because if it is – well, we can
clear this thing up right now and I can go home and go
jogging and rushing off to the DIY centre.

STEPHANIE: You're alright, Colin; you're just a bit
over-excited.

COLIN: Yeah.

STEPHANIE: And depressed.

COLIN: Ah yes. Well, who isn't? After all, hm? You say
to me 'Are you depressed' I say 'Who isn't?' But maybe
I'm wrong – maybe people aren't! Maybe they're not.
But I've always assumed they are. The news reader is
depressed, but you'd expect that, all the terrible things
she has to read out. Oh! Terrible, terrible, terrible. That
Lebanon! Oh! She knows all about it and she comes in
and she tries to tell me. Me especially. She thinks she's
telling tales. Telling tales about Lebanon and multi-
murderers and – but I've got to know, haven't I? It's for
my own good.

TONY is standing up.

MADDY: Where are you off to, Tony?

COLIN: Going for a slash. Could be a crap. Only time will tell.

MADDY: Can he, um… It's not funny actually, Stephanie.

STEPHANIE: Sorry, I know; it's just the way he put it.

COLIN: (*To MADDY.*) You mean can he crap? God; yes. It's not like talking, is it? Otherwise I'd never be out of the bog. And no writing on the walls.

TONY goes off. COLIN lapses into silence.

(*Suddenly, with a loud clap of hands.*) Right!

STEPHANIE: (*Jumping.*) Oh! I wish you wouldn't do that!

MADDY: Oh, I nearly jumped out of my skin then.

COLIN: I thought he'd never go. Now can we really talk about him, Whatdyathink?

MADDY: Are you looking after him, are you?

COLIN: Me? I don't know really.

MADDY: Do you feed him?

COLIN: Feed him? No. They do that. Sometimes he can manage. Especially when it's curry; he likes that.

MADDY: (*To STEPHANIE.*) Ooh, can you imagine the curry here! Don't you think he's lost weight though, Steph?

STEPHANIE: He has but he'll put it back on.

COLIN: He'll have to find it first, won't he?

MADDY: Anyway I was right not to bring the kids. God!

COLIN: Kids are nice, though, aren't they? They come in here and they say, 'What's wrong with Mum?' 'Why is that man peeing down his leg, Mum?'

MADDY: He doesn't pee himself, does he? Colin?

COLIN: Hm?

MADDY: Tony – he doesn't pee himself?

COLIN: He couldn't pee someone else, could he?

STEPHANIE laughs.

MADDY: You're making him worse, d'you realise that?

STEPHANIE: I know, it's terrible, but I can't help it. It's just the way he says things all of a sudden.

MADDY: He's doing it deliberately.

STEPHANIE: Maybe he is: I just find it impossible to tell.

COLIN: My wife doesn't understand me.

MADDY: Was that funny as well?

STEPHANIE: No, it's just once you start, you know.

COLIN: What have I said now? I know I'm obtuse.

STEPHANIE: Obtuse. You certainly are.

MADDY: You know very well I don't know the meaning of that bloody word.

COLIN: Well then, you won't guess it. It sounds like fat but it doesn't mean that.

MADDY: Actually, what I was trying to get from you, if you don't mind, was some important information. It may not be important to either of you, but it is to me.

COLIN: Ah yes. Well then, you were quite right to ask. What did you ask?

MADDY: Does Tony wet himself?

COLIN: Well, only if he has to.

STEPHANIE laughs.

– I don't know why she's laughing.

MADDY: Why-should-he-have-to?

COLIN: Because – the mountain doesn't always come to Mohammed.

MADDY: I see. Because he can't always get to the loo. Why not? Why can't he get to the loo?

COLIN: He's afraid.

MADDY: Oh really, yes? And what's he afraid of?

COLIN: Some terrible things happen in the toilets. I don't know if it's the same in the ladies. I expect they do, but in a more genteel way.

MADDY: Have you any idea what he's talking about?

STEPHANIE: Absolutely none.

COLIN: I'm mad.

MADDY: No, but you're able to have a laugh at me, aren't you? Terrible things happen in the toilets? What on earth are you talking about?

COLIN: Well, it's the lights and everything echoes. A lot of us go in the bushes with the insects. Looking up at the stars with that patter-patter sound. Hawkeye and his faithful Indian companion – what a beautiful relationship that was. Very mature. There's a stream out there. We paddle in it; paddle and piddle. After that it goes down to the sea through caves measureless to man. Such reading I've been doing in here, Steph. I'll tell you about it when I... I'm ever so cultured really. (*Cockney.*) Well, makes a change, dunnit? See I been 'eld back in me life, haven't I?

MADDY: Well, I don't know what you're talking about but that's another thing I'm going to find out about. There's nothing so undignified for a man.

COLIN: Yes. As what?

STEPHANIE: I'm sure he doesn't, Maddy?

COLIN: He doesn't what? Who? (*He looks from one to the other.*) I do. When I can. Which is often. (*Holds his head and cries out.*) Owww! (*Simpering voice.*) 'Medicine time, Colin, medicine time, Colin.'

MADDY: And that's another thing I don't like: all these first-names they use. How are they going to learn to hold their heads up when they've got young nurses calling them by their first names?

COLIN: Yes. Well, first names come first; I don't know if that's any help. I don't suppose they have time to learn your second name. (*To STEPHANIE.*) Do you think?

STEPHANIE: Probably, love.

COLIN: Yeah. Alright, Mad? Oh, mustn't call you that, must I? Be keeping you in. (*He laughs. Calls off.*) *Alright,* boys? See you at the disco. Don't forget the Saturday Night Fever, eh? I'm trying to teach it to them, you know, the routine, but the trouble is their colostomy bags get in the way.

STEPHANIE laughs.

MADDY: (*To STEPHANIE.*) Do you think that's funny?

STEPHANIE: Well, I do really, yes.

MADDY: Yes, isn't it funny how people's sense of humour is different.

STEPHANIE: Well, it's just the context, you know.

MADDY: Oh, is it, yes.

COLIN: What we have here is a lunatic context. What we are we heavily into here is fantasy...

MADDY: Yeah well, I'm not in the mood, Colin...

COLIN: Take me for example; I don't fantasise about being Napoleon or anything; I don't fancy I'm living other people's lives – if anything it's those bastards out there who are leading mine. I see someone drive past in his car – that bastard is leading my life! And he's not looking well on it. I want to say to him OI COME BACK HERE, YOU PUKE...

MADDY: (*Covering her ears.*) Oh, please!

COLIN: They lead my life but they don't do anything with it, there ought to be a law against it. In fact that's not a bad idea. (*To STEPHANIE.*) Miss Jameson, take a letter! I must look into all this stuff, build up a file on it. Or perhaps you can while you're – have you got a lover?

STEPHANIE: Have I?

COLIN: Yeah, have you?

STEPHANIE: No.

COLIN: Why not?

STEPHANIE: I'm waiting for you to come home, aren't I?

COLIN: Why don't you have one while you're waiting?

STEPHANIE: I don't know.

COLIN: Attractive woman like you. I mean it's different for her.

MADDY: Oh, thank you very much.

COLIN: Anyway take one, as they say. You can pretend it's me, if you're desperate. It probably *is* me.
BASTARD!

MADDY: (*Covering her ears.*) Oh, I can't take this...

COLIN: What does he do for a living anyway? What's his name? How much does he pay you?

STEPHANIE: It hasn't happened.

COLIN: He hasn't paid you yet?

STEPHANIE: I haven't got a lover.

COLIN: I thought you said you had.

STEPHANIE: No. You asked me if I had; I said no; you agreed the answer was yes. You talked yourself into it.

COLIN: We said all that?

STEPHANIE: Yes.

COLIN: Shit, that was almost a conversation we had, wasn't it?

STEPHANIE: It was a conversation.

COLIN: But I do that, you see; that's very – of you. But I do do that. Sometimes I might be right, though.

STEPHANIE: Sometimes, but not this time.

COLIN: So you're just waiting for me to come home, are you? Doesn't sound like a lot of fun.

STEPHANIE: It isn't.

COLIN: Attractive woman like you.

STEPHANIE: Yes.

COLIN: You should sing, dance, ha-cha-cha.

STEPHANIE: I know.

COLIN: I mean I could – choose. I could so – choose, any time I like, to get better and pull my finger out. I'm only malingering, you know. I'm after sympathy. Tea and tarts and lots of sympathy. How d'you think I'm doing? See, I just talk, really. I don't do anything dangerous.

STEPHANIE: We know that.

COLIN: I'm not like him. He's a real nutter. Your husband, Missis. We shouldn't be in the same place, except I'm supposed to be good for him.

STEPHANIE: You are.

MADDY: Huh.

COLIN: I could walk out of here now and no one would give me a second look. Take up my rightful place in – don't you agree?

STEPHANIE: Maybe.

COLIN: Yeah, it's just an act, you see. I mean this is mad. (*Makes a series of crazy faces.*) I get carried away sometimes, that's all.

STEPHANIE: What about this library job?

COLIN: Library? You got a job in a library?

STEPHANIE: No, you said you put the books in the fridge, that's all.

COLIN: Did they tell you that?

Pause.

She looks at him.

MADDY: It's the drugs; that's how they work.

COLIN: I don't take drugs.

STEPHANIE: You're just a bit forgetful, that's all.

COLIN: I remember things – no one else ever remembers. Your footprint in the sand in Madeira.

STEPHANIE: Yes, I know.

COLIN: You see him over there? Petey. Silly sod went and laid this enormous great table when we had a cricket game. Us against the ambulance drivers. It took him over an hour to lay it, laid everything out really beautifully, very intricate. Stood back and admired it. Then he realised he hadn't put a table-cloth on and so he took everything off the table, put the table-cloth on and started re-laying it. They had to have their teas on their knees. Now *that* is really forgetful. (*To MADDY.*) Whatdyathink?

MADDY: It's sad.

COLIN: No, I mean about me. What do you think about me?

MADDY: I can't say, Colin.

COLIN: Why not? Cat got your tongue?

MADDY: I don't think it's right for me to say.

COLIN: Go on, live. You're amongst friends. Much may depend upon your answer.

MADDY: I know. That just makes it all the more difficult, doesn't it?

COLIN: Ah.

MADDY: I think you're very sharp and original.

COLIN: Ah yes.

He studies her for some time.

– So who's trying to kill you these days?

MADDY: What?

STEPHANIE: Oh, come on, Colin – sit down.

COLIN: What?

STEPHANIE: Sit down!

COLIN: What did I say? I only said who's she seeing now?

STEPHANIE: You may think you said that.

MADDY: Oh, he knows what he said.

COLIN: Oh, I see. I said something else, did I? Shit. You can't rely on anything, can you? Not even your own voice.

STEPHANIE: Tony was not trying to kill Maddy, alright?

MADDY: Oh, it's alright, leave it.

STEPHANIE: I want him to understand. Do you understand?

COLIN: Yes. He wasn't. It was a cry for help.

STEPHANIE: Well, we don't know *what* it was. He was schizophrenic.

COLIN: Hm. I've never known what that word means. Like 'alienated' – I've never known what that means either. Life's a sod, isn't it? You versus terminology over fifteen rounds.

STEPHANIE: (*Seriously.*) That's quite amusing, Colin.

COLIN: Is it?

STEPHANIE: Yes.

COLIN: (*To MADDY.*) She loves me really, you know.

MADDY: You're lucky then, aren't you?

COLIN: Yeah. But I just get depressed, and these queer notions. God, I'm tired.

MADDY: I'm not surprised. I think they should have a rest in the afternoons: I think these visiting hours are too long.

COLIN: Yeah, we get very stimulated. By you especially. That reminds me; there's a man over there, you see him? He can't stop masturbating. He's been watching you ever since you arrived. Have you noticed him? He's

the one with the grin and the very red face. It's not just you; he does it all the time. They're thinking of fitting him up with a device, but – Oh! I've just remembered a dream
I had last night!

He clutches his head and remembers the dreams. He moans again.

STEPHANIE: Why don't you go and see if Tony's alright?

COLIN: Me? Yeah, okay. Where is he?

STEPHANIE: He went to the loo, remember?

COLIN: Oh yes. He spews a lot in the afternoons.

MADDY: Oh God.

STEPHANIE: Well, go and see if he's okay and bring him back. Because we can't stay long.

COLIN: Right then. I'll just go and say hello to Wanker…

He goes.

The two women sit in silence. They each light a cigarette.

MADDY: He spews in the afternoons? Do you believe it? What are we going to do about them?

STEPHANIE: I don't know. Maybe you ought to take him out of here. Go private.

MADDY: I don't know. It sounds awful but… (*She stops.*)

STEPHANIE: (*Looking after COLIN.*) Now he's gone – all the life has gone. Don't you feel it?

MADDY: He'd drive me mad. But I mean, how can you imagine them, walking around like that? God knows how long it was inside them before – how long was it lingering, this sickness? I'm going to start the divorce, Steph. I know it sounds hard, but this is not the man I married.

STEPHANIE: No.

MADDY: I mean I've got to think of myself, and the kids. I mean it's all very well, this. How many women would put up with a man who said he wanted to kill her? You tell me that. How can anyone go on with a person like that? Colin says nice things to you – okay, maybe he doesn't mean them, but it's nice to hear them. Have you seen Tony's face when he looks at me? I feel as though it's the devil, I do.

STEPHANIE: Why should he feel that way about you?

MADDY: Fuck knows.

STEPHANIE: What have you done to him?

MADDY: What have I *done* to him? Oh, only cooked his meals, washed his clothes, raised his kids for him. While he went off and pursued his career. That's what I've done for him.

STEPHANIE: No, I know, but – I'm just trying to work it out, that's all. Is there anything you've stopped him doing?

MADDY: I've obviously not made myself clear. I've been his wife. I've raised his kids…

STEPHANIE: Yeah, I know but…

MADDY: It's not a question of 'but', is it? I've done all those things. I know what you're talking about; I'm not stupid. It's all sex, isn't it? That rules everything these days. But what I say is this. How many women keep the taste for it through eleven years, just exactly the same? Anyway, you don't expect your husband to want to murder you. It's not always your fault, don't forget. Christ knows it's not. I don't know why you're looking at me like that. I don't know what it is you think I've said. It's them who have to do the explaining, not

me. It's for them to tell me why he's the way he is. I'm
not the mad one. Tell you the truth, I'm almost past
caring. Certify him and stay with the kids. He'll have
no authority over them. Once you've shown you're
mentally unstable – that's it; you cannot come within
a mile of them. I know it sounds hard, but why's he in
here? Because he wanted to kill his wife. It's all very
well, isn't it? Being 'understanding', but I'm not going to
put my head in
a noose, am I?

STEPHANIE: I don't think he was trying to kill you.

MADDY: Well, I beg to differ, and I don't know any other
woman who'd hang around to find out. It's alright for
you; Colin'll be back to normal soon, and you can take
him out.

STEPHANIE: I'd never realised how funny he could be.

MADDY: Oh, he's funny alright.

STEPHANIE: How he could make me laugh. My father
could always do that. And not much makes me laugh.
I never laugh at jokes. I worshipped the ground he
walked on, you know.

MADDY: Who, Colin?

STEPHANIE: No, my father.

MADDY: Oh. Well, that's normal, isn't it? Even if they're
bastards.

Pause.

The sun comes over again; STEPHANIE basks in it.

STEPHANIE: Divorce, yes. I do see, Maddy.

MADDY: It's fair enough, isn't it?

STEPHANIE: It's fair if it's what you want. Why does everything – get darker? It starts out bright, with four people on holiday learning a dance and ends up…

MADDY: With him trying to kill me.

STEPHANIE: I don't think he was trying to kill you.

MADDY: It's alright for you to say that. Whose side are you on anyway? We're supposed to stick together, or haven't you heard?

STEPHANIE: Who is?

MADDY: Women.

STEPHANIE: Oh, yes. It's just that I would have thought, if he'd really wanted to do it he would have done it.

MADDY: Oh yeah, great, thanks a lot. That's great grounds for marriage, isn't it? You'll say we should be sleeping in the same room next.

STEPHANIE: How long have…

MADDY: Ah, I *knew* you were going to say that – the moment I let that slip, I knew you'd say 'how long have you been sleeping apart?'

STEPHANIE: I'm sorry to be so predictable.

MADDY: Since you ask – six years. Okay?

STEPHANIE: Six years?

MADDY: Ever since I had Chloe.

STEPHANIE: Do you, I mean do…?

MADDY: No, we don't.

STEPHANIE: Doesn't he want to?

MADDY: With me? Don't know. Doubt it.

STEPHANIE: Don't you fancy him?

MADDY: Sometimes I think you're immature, Stephanie. Of course I 'fancy' him, as you put it. Sometimes. There's no one else to fancy, is there? You seen round us? It's all walking-frames and deaf-aids. That dirty old man is looking at me. (*Shouts at him.*) Go on! Shoo! Oh, I think I'm going to see the doctor; I can't get it off my mind.

But she lingers.

STEPHANIE: What's the matter?

MADDY: I'm going to ask him about the divorce.

STEPHANIE: I know.

MADDY: I think I better had, don't you?

STEPHANIE: If it's what you want you better had.

MADDY: I'm sure he'll understand. They must be used to it. I mean I'll tell him I'll see it through; keep visiting him, sort of thing. Okay then. You'll be alright?

STEPHANIE: I'll be alright.

MADDY goes. STEPHANIE is alone.

Feel quite at home actually.

It is getting darker, slowly.

TONY returns. He sits down. He says nothing for a while.

TONY: Where's Colin?

STEPHANIE: He went looking for you.

Pause.

Are you alright?

TONY: Yeah.

STEPHANIE: Why are you talking now?

TONY: I haven't said much, have I?

STEPHANIE: No, but you've…

TONY: Feel like it.

STEPHANIE: What, and you didn't before?

TONY: No.

STEPHANIE: Why don't you talk to Madeleine?

TONY: Don't know.

STEPHANIE: Colin says you talk all the time.

TONY: With him around that'd be difficult.

STEPHANIE: Don't you think Madeleine would like to have a talk with you? She's very upset. She thinks you don't want to see her.

TONY: I bet I get out of here before Colin does.

STEPHANIE: What makes you say that?

TONY: I do, that's all.

STEPHANIE: That's not a very nice thing to say, is it? To his wife.

Pause.

I mean why do you say it?

TONY: 'Cos it's true.

STEPHANIE: How do you know?

TONY: I don't say 'I know'; I say 'I bet'.

STEPHANIE: Well, I don't think there's very much wrong with Colin. And as a matter of fact, I'm going to take him home today.

TONY: You can't do that; he's mad?

STEPHANIE: What do you mean by 'mad'?

TONY: Is that what he's told you? He's alright?

STEPHANIE: No, I've deduced it.

TONY: You've deduced it. I deduce different.

STEPHANIE: On what evidence? You haven't given me any reason to believe you.

TONY: I don't have to.

STEPHANIE: Just because you resent him. Why should you begrudge him going out if you both come out eventually?

TONY: He's worse than me and you can see the state I'm in.

STEPHANIE: What state are you in?

TONY: What do you think?

STEPHANIE: I don't know.

TONY: You know about him, though.

STEPHANIE: I know him better than you.

TONY: Do you?

STEPHANIE: Maybe you just want Maddy to think you're in a state.

TONY: You think I'd go to all this trouble just for that?

STEPHANIE: No.

TONY: Yeah well, try thinking before you speak.

STEPHANIE: You seem very rational all of a sudden.

TONY: I've never stopped being 'rational'. What you mean is I'm argumentative.

STEPHANIE: You certainly are that.

TONY: I'm just making it up as I go along. That's what all mad people do. It's quite frightening. But I'll tell you something: I don't think we're the only ones.

STEPHANIE: But we get on with our lives, don't we?

TONY: Oh yes, you do that.

STEPHANIE: Because we have to.

TONY: Bloody women. What do you want – a medal?

STEPHANIE: No…

TONY: There are some bloody female heroes out there. All getting on with it, and crowing to each other how they can do it better than men. Well, why don't you all go off to some fucking island somewhere and leave us in peace?

STEPHANIE: Maybe we will.

TONY: Can't be too soon for me.

STEPHANIE: Why don't you tell Maddy you love her?

TONY: You've not been listening to me, have you?

STEPHANIE: Yes, I've been listening.

TONY: But you don't believe me? Because I'm in here. You want to tell her that, you tell her.

STEPHANIE: A husband is supposed to tell his wife things like that, isn't he?

TONY: Yeah well, I don't do what I'm *supposed* to do, do I?

STEPHANIE: You talk a lot when you get going, don't you?

TONY: Yeah, I'm going, but where to?

STEPHANIE: That's up to you, isn't it?

TONY: It isn't; it's up to them. They've got to stop telling me lies.

STEPHANIE: No one's telling you lies.

TONY: They do. The police do. Down the telephones.

STEPHANIE: What police?

TONY: There's only one police, isn't there? The ones that ring me up.

STEPHANIE: Do they ring you or do you ring them?

TONY: Typical question, that is. What difference does it make?

STEPHANIE: Why are you sick in the afternoons?

TONY: Isn't everybody?

STEPHANIE: I'm not.

TONY: You wouldn't be. Mess your nice tidy floor. You think I'm funny?

STEPHANIE: Not a bit.

TONY: I do. I think I'm hilarious. I kill myself. That's why they take away my shoelaces and belt, because I kill myself.

STEPHANIE: Okay, I agree; you're hilarious.

TONY: Why aren't you laughing then?

STEPHANIE: I don't show my feelings very well.

TONY: That's a fault.

STEPHANIE: I know.

TONY: That can land you in deep shit. That can land you in here. Have you seen the women? Breaks your heart. (*He eats a jam tart.*) Nice.

STEPHANIE: She brought them for you.

TONY: They're having a disco later.

STEPHANIE: Yes, I know.

TONY: You can pick a partner.

STEPHANIE: I've already got one.

TONY: I expect you feel you're being a bit patronising.

STEPHANIE: Maybe.

TONY: Definitely.

STEPHANIE: I'm sorry; it's not often I've had the experience of speaking to people who've been certified.

TONY: They used to come down and poke sticks at us, didn't they? Sunday afternoons in Bedlam, you know? I think that was probably quite healthy, really. For you, not for us. Talking to certified people is just the same as talking to normal people; you just have to learn to change the subject quickly.

STEPHANIE: Yes, you do jump about a lot.

TONY: I'm eating all these.

STEPHANIE: That's what they're for. Why are you here, Tony?

TONY: Why are any of us here?

STEPHANIE: Now you're being patronising.

TONY: Why am I here? I'm here because you asked me that question.

STEPHANIE: What question?

TONY: You are following me, aren't you? The question 'Why are you here?' If I hadn't been here you wouldn't have asked it. How could you because I wouldn't have been here?

STEPHANIE: Why do you want to kill Maddy?

TONY: Doesn't everybody?

STEPHANIE: Definitely not.

TONY: Well, perhaps they would if they thought about it. People don't think, you see. I thought it was a good idea... Trouble was, no one seemed to agree with me. (*He shrugs.*) Can't argue, I suppose.

STEPHANIE: But why did it seem like a good idea?

TONY: Because she was there. I've a good mind to go back into my shell again.

STEPHANIE: Is it nice in there? In the shell?

TONY: No, it isn't. I've always been attracted to people who talk a lot. I think they're more trustworthy, on the whole.

STEPHANIE: Women talk a lot, don't they?

TONY: Oh yeah, they 'talk'.

STEPHANIE: Is that why you like Colin?

TONY: Who says I like him?

STEPHANIE: He's trying to help you.

TONY: He should help himself. Tell you what, I don't think I'm a very interesting person really. I don't know why they waste their journeys on me.

STEPHANIE: Perhaps they won't much longer. Perhaps you'll have no visitors whatsoever.

TONY: I don't think you're saying any of the correct things to me. I don't think they'd approve your approach.

STEPHANIE: I'm not a psychiatrist. I'm just making it up as I go along. Besides I think you've got a fucking cheek, making out you want to kill your wife.

TONY: Yeah, I have got a cheek.

STEPHANIE: Yes well, it's time you smartened up, isn't it?

TONY: It's time I did a lot of things.

STEPHANIE: If you feel nothing for her leave her in peace.

TONY: Peace?

STEPHANIE: Yes.

TONY: You know all about that, I suppose? Peace?

STEPHANIE: You can talk like this to me. Say something to her, or leave her alone.

TONY: My own wife?

STEPHANIE: What?

TONY: Leave my own wife?

STEPHANIE: It does happen you know.

TONY: I think that's sick. It's completely out of the question. We're married. Better or worse; sickness and health. This is the worse and sickness bit. Too fucking bad. We're married. I don't know what's the matter with you women – you talk so easily about walking out on your responsibilities and giving yourself more choice and all that. What I say is – let's have a bit of respect here. Let's have a bit of consistency, of seeing a thing through. You know what I mean?

STEPHANIE: Not really.

TONY: I mean you've got no morals. You give up too easily…

STEPHANIE: Huh! So she's supposed to sit there while you…

TONY: Yeah, that's exactly what she's supposed to do. Anyone can walk out of a door, like my father did, like everyone does these days. I'm here, aren't I? Seeing it through? It's the least she can do.

STEPHANIE: I feel as though I'm going out of my mind…

COLIN rushes on.

COLIN: Ah well, you're in the right place, aren't you?

He ruffles TONY's hair.

– Alright, Tone? You been talking about me?

STEPHANIE: No, we haven't.

COLIN: Oh. Well, what on earth have you been talking about? You eaten all these jam tarts, you scumbag? When's the disco going to start? It's getting dark.

STEPHANIE: My God, you're all like children. What am I going to do? I've led all my life in the dark, asleep.

COLIN: What do you say? What did she say?

STEPHANIE: I never thought of you as amusing, but you do make me laugh, you fool.

COLIN: (*With his mouth full of cake.*) I used to make you laugh when we made love.

STEPHANIE: (*Smiling.*) Anyway…

COLIN: It's just a face we're going through. (*Makes a crazy face.*) If I was a raving thing like that they could fix me up, couldn't they? But what I've got is very subtle, you see; it's very modern, very now; it's in the Sunday papers. It declines to come out and show its fangs; it just sits back and bides its time. Many might be afraid it will one day spring out and go WOO-HA!

He does it right in STEPHANIE's face. She doesn't flinch.

STEPHANIE: It doesn't have to do that, does it?

COLIN: Well, there's no law on the subject. Unless they make one before I get out of here. (*To TONY.*) My wife's got a lot of faith in me.

TONY: They all have.

COLIN: Yes. He doesn't like women much. He's not convinced of their necessity. But what I say is – where would we be without 'em? I mean bless their 'earts.

STEPHANIE: I'm going to take you home today.

COLIN: Yeah? What's for tea?

STEPHANIE: You'll have to wait and see, won't you?

COLIN: You going to bust me out?

STEPHANIE: If need be.

COLIN: Why don't you take one of them? Old Wanker. Take him.

STEPHANIE: I'm taking you.

COLIN: They won't let you.

STEPHANIE: We're going home.

COLIN: Can we go to the disco first?

STEPHANIE: If you like.

COLIN: YAHOO!

TONY: What about me?

COLIN: You'll have to wait your turn.

TONY: There aren't any 'turns'.

COLIN: See, I just get depressed and then – you know…

STEPHANIE: I know.

COLIN: I mean I can't really say I'm *well.*

STEPHANIE: No, you're not well. But you're not this ill.

COLIN: Well, I'm not as ill as him. And I do open my zip to pee.

She laughs. They kiss. This is too much for TONY.

TONY: (*Baying.*) WHERE'S MY WIFE?

COLIN: She's coming...

TONY: WHERE'S MY WIFE?

COLIN: Ssh, it's alright...

TONY: I WANT MY WIFE...

TONY starts to have a fit. COLIN slaps his face in a practised way. This calms him only momentarily. His fit continues. Finally COLIN holds him very firmly and they stay like this until he quietens. STEPHANIE watches the whole thing, aghast. COLIN lets go of him. He ruffles his hair. He's alright.

The music starts. The fairy lights come on – it's pretty dark by now. They recognise the song. It is from 'Saturday Night Fever' (The theme song). They get up and start to dance: COLIN, STEPHANIE and TONY. They dance in perfect formation – the routine they learned on holiday, years ago.

Some way in, MADDY returns. She stands watching, despondent. But after a while she joins in. The four of them dance in formation, not touching, and some distance from each other. The women laugh: the men concentrate on the moves.

Lights down; the music continues.

The End.

WWW.OBERONBOOKS.COM

www.ingramcontent.com/pod-product-compliance
Ingram Content Group UK Ltd.
Pitfield, Milton Keynes, MK11 3LW, UK
UKHW020722280225
455688UK00012B/471